DRIVING STANDARDS AGENCY

GW00721928

DRIVING SKILLS

THE OFFICIAL

THEORY TEST
for Large
Vehicle Drivers

including the questions and answers

London: The Stationery Office

Written and compiled by the Publications Unit of the
Driving Standards Agency

Questions and answers written and compiled by the
National Foundation for Educational Research

Illustrations by Vicky Squires
Designed, edited and published by The Stationery Office Limited

© Crown Copyright 1996
Published with the permission of the Driving Standards Agency on behalf
of the Controller of Her Majesty's Stationery Office.

Applications for reproduction should be made in writing to
The Copyright Unit, Her Majesty's Stationery Office, St Clements,
2–16 Colegate, Norwich NR3 1BQ.

The Stationery Office Limited is a new publishing company in the private sector.
Many titles previously published by HMSO – an Executive Agency of the
Cabinet Office – will in future be published by The Stationery Office Limited.
Contact The Stationery Office Limited for further information.

ISBN 0 11 551780 4

British Library Cataloguing in Publication Data
A CIP catalogue record for this book is available from the British Library.

Acknowledgements

The Driving Standards Agency would like to thank the following
for their assistance

National Foundation for Educational Research

Transport Research Laboratory

Department of Transport Road Safety Division

The staff of the Driving Standards Agency

The staff of the Driver & Vehicle Testing Agency (Northern Ireland)

Every effort has been made to ensure that the information contained in this
publication is accurate at the time of going to press. The Stationery Office
Limited cannot be held responsible for any inaccuracies. Information in this book
is for guidance only.

The Driving Standards Agency (DSA) is an Executive Agency of the Department of Transport. You'll see its logo at test centres.

DRIVING
STANDARDS
AGENCY

"Safe driving for life"

The aim of the DSA is to promote road safety through the advancement of driving standards.

DSA

- Conducts practical driving tests for drivers or riders of cars, motorcycles, lorries, buses and other vehicles

- Plans, maintains and supervises the theory test for drivers or riders of cars, motorcycles, lorries and buses

- Controls the register of Approved Driving Instructors (ADIs)

- Supervises Compulsory Basic Training (CBT) courses for motorcyclists

- Aims to provide a high-quality service to its customers

DVTA

The Driver & Vehicle Testing Agency (DVTA) is an Executive Agency within the Department of the Environment for Northern Ireland. Its primary aim is to promote and improve road safety through the advancement of driving standards and the implementation of the Government's policies for improving the mechanical standards of vehicles.

To be considered 'professional' in the true sense of the word, the driver of a large goods (LGV) or passenger carrying vehicle (PCV) must have a high degree of vehicle handling skills. He or she also must have knowledge and a clear understanding of the principles of safe driving and how to apply them. Whether you're responsible for the safe transportation of goods or passengers, the need for comprehensive knowledge is recognised by the introduction of a separate theory test. This is a major initiative aimed at improving road safety standards in the UK.

Passing the theory test is an important step in becoming a professional driver. When you drive a large vehicle you should demonstrate your ability to drive safely and set a good example to others on the road. Your attitude and approach should be courteous and considerate. The safety of the goods or passengers you carry could depend on it.

This book will help you to prepare for your theory test. It contains the questions, set out in an easy-to-read style with plenty of illustrations. To aid learning, it explains why the answers are correct and identifies good driving practices.

There are other books in the Driving Skills series that will help you to develop your skills.

The Driving Manual
The Goods Vehicle Driving Manual
The Bus and Coach Driving Manual

All are published by The Stationery Office and will provide you with valuable information.

Robin Cummins
The Chief Driving Examiner
Driving Standards Agency

This book will help you to

▶ **Study for your theory test**
▶ **Prepare and help you to pass**

Part One will give you information on how to get started.

Part Two will tell you about the question paper and how to answer it.

Part Three will show you the questions that might be used on your test. Don't worry, you won't have to answer all of them. Your paper will have 25 questions.

The questions are in the left-hand column with the answers beneath. On the right of the page you'll find a brief explanation of why the answers are correct.

To become a professional driver you must have a thorough knowledge of the regulations that apply to your work. The questions in the theory test will test you on this knowledge. Combined with a high level of driving skill, this will ensure that you carry out your work safely.

If you're driving a passenger carrying vehicle (PCV) you'll be providing a service to paying customers. These passengers have been entrusted into your care. You should be aware of this and the responsibility it carries.

If you're driving a large goods vehicle (LGV) you must ensure that your goods arrive at their destination safely. This process will not only involve the safety of your load but also your attitude to others on the road. From the start, you must be aware of the differences between driving smaller vehicles and driving large buses or lorries.

Buy a copy of *The Highway Code* and read it thoroughly. You must have a sound knowledge of *The Highway Code,* including the meaning of traffic signs and road markings. You must be especially aware of those that indicate a restriction for lorries or buses.

The Stationery Office (formerly part of HMSO) publishes books in the Driving Skills series on behalf of the DSA. *The Goods Vehicle Driving Manual* and *The Bus and Coach Driving Manual* are highly recommended. Information given in these books will help you to answer the theory test questions. You'll find these books in all good bookshops. There are also books about driving available from other publishers.

If you want to drive a large goods vehicle (LGV)

You must apply to the Driver and Vehicle and Licensing Agency (DVLA) in Swansea for the provisional entitlement to drive large goods vehicles. An application form D1 is available from post offices. In Northern Ireland the equivalent form DL1 is available from post offices and from Driver and Vehicle Licensing Northern Ireland (DVLNI) in Coleraine.

In order to drive an LGV you must

- Have a full driving licence for category B vehicles
- Hold a provisional LGV driving licence
- Meet the eyesight and medical requirements
- Normally be over 21 years old

Full details can be obtained from the DVLA enquiry line on 0179 277 2151. In Northern Ireland phone the DVLNI on 01265 41200.

When you have your provisional licence you must

- Sign it
- Only drive under the supervision of a person over the age of 21 who has had a full licence for three years and holds a full UK LGV licence for the category of vehicle being driven
- Display L plates (or D plates, if you wish, when driving in Wales) at the front and rear of the vehicle
- Display LGV/PCV plates to the front and rear of the vehicle when driving in Northern Ireland

You'll have to be fully qualified in a lower category of entitlement before seeking to gain entitlement in a higher category or sub-category. You'll have to

- Pass a category C test before taking a category C + E test
- Pass a category C or C1 test before taking a category C1 + E test

You won't have to gain category C1 before taking a test in category C.

If you want to drive a bus or coach (PCV)

Buses and coaches are referred to as passenger carrying vehicles (PCVs).

You must apply to the DVLA for the provisional entitlement to drive a PCV. An application form D1 is available from post offices.

In order to drive a PCV you must

- Have a full driving licence for category B vehicles
- Hold a provisional PCV licence
- Meet the eyesight and medical requirements
- Normally be over 21 years old

Full details can be obtained from the DVLA enquiry line on 0179 277 2151. In Northern Ireland phone the DVLNI on 01265 41200.

When you have your provisional licence you must

- Sign it
- Only drive under the supervision of a person over the age of 21 who has held a full licence for three years and a licence for the category of vehicle being driven

- Display L plates (or D plates, if you wish, when driving in Wales) at the front and rear of the vehicle
- Display LGV/PCV plates to the front and rear of the vehicle when driving in Northern Ireland

You'll have to be fully qualified in the lower category of entitlement before seeking to gain entitlement in a higher category. You'll have to

- Pass a category D test before taking a category D + E test
- Pass a category D or D1 test before taking a category D1 + E test

You won't have to pass a test for a D1 (minibus) category before taking a test in category D.

Medical requirements

You'll be responsible for goods or passengers so it's vital that you meet exacting medical standards. The medical requirements apply for both LGV and PCV licences.

You can't hold an LGV or PCV licence unless your eyesight meets the high standard required.

You must be fit and free from any condition that affects your ability to retain control of a large vehicle. If you're disabled you may drive a vehicle that has been especially adapted for you.

If this is your first application for either an LGV or a PCV licence you must have a medical. This must be carried out by a doctor. The medical report form D4 (DLM1 in Northern Ireland) must be completed and submitted with your licence application form.

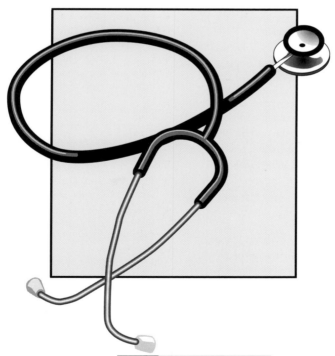

Ready for your test?

Make sure that you're well prepared before you attempt the test. Good preparation will save you time and money.

DriveSafe Services Ltd conducts theory tests on behalf of the DSA and the DVTA. There are over 150 theory test centres throughout Great Britain and Northern Ireland.

Theory test sessions are available during weekdays, evenings and on Saturdays. A test appointment will normally be available for you within about two weeks of your preferred date.

You can find out where your local centre is from

- A driver-training organisation
- A DSA or DVTA driving test centre
- The telephone information line 0645 000 555

How to book your test

If you're training with a driver-training organisation they'll probably book your test for you. Otherwise you can get an application form from

- A DSA or DVTA driving test centre
- Your local DSA Area Office

The easiest way to book your test is by phone, using your credit or debit card. If you book by this method you'll be given the date and time of your test immediately. You can do this by phoning 0645 000 666 at any time between 8 am and 6 pm Monday to Friday. When you ring you should have ready your

- DVLA licence number
- Credit or debit card details

For a Minicom machine ring 0645 700 301. Welsh speakers can call 0645 700 201.

The question paper is available in the following languages

English
Welsh
Bengali
Urdu
Punjabi
Chinese
Gujerati
Hindi

If you can speak English but can't read in the languages provided a member of staff will be available to read through the test on a one-to-one basis. State this on your application form or tell the operator when you call to book your test.

If you can't read or write any of the languages available you're allowed to bring a translator with you when you take your test. You can only bring a translator who's approved as independent and a member of a suitable professional institute, such as The Institute of Translation and Interpreting (ITT) or The Institute of Linguists. The enquiry operator will be able to tell you about these or other approved organisations. You should inform the booking office that you intend to bring a translator with you when you take your theory test.

If you're dyslexic or have difficulty reading, don't worry. If it's necessary, you'll be allowed double the normal time to take the test. If you have extreme difficulties, a reader can be provided. You'll normally have to provide a statement to confirm that extra time is needed.

Every effort has been made to ensure that the theory test can be taken by all candidates. Telephone the theory test information line for more details.

To ensure that all candidates are tested fairly, questions used in the theory test will be under constant review. A few of the questions will be changed periodically to reflect changes in legislation or as a result of customer feedback.

If you take a theory test you may find questions that don't appear in this book. The information needed to answer them is readily available in the series of Driving Skills books and *The Highway Code.*

Transitional arrangements

After 1 July 1997 it will be necessary to pass the theory test before a booking for a practical test will be accepted. However, between 1 January and 30 June 1997 there will be a special arrangement to allow you to take the practical test first, if necessary. In this case, to gain a full licence the theory test must be taken and passed within six months.

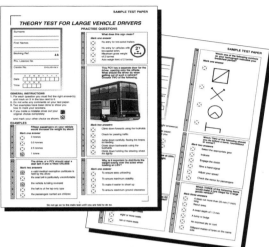

The question paper will have 25 questions. You should attempt to answer all of them.

There will be different types of question in the paper. Most of them will ask you to mark ONE correct answer from four. Other questions will ask you for TWO or more correct answers from a selection.

Some of the questions will show you a picture. These are to test your knowledge of traffic signs or your ability to recognise hazards. Look at them carefully. Mark the box alongside the answer(s) you think is/are correct.

On the front of the question paper there are some practise questions. You'll be given the chance to attempt these before the test begins.

Some questions will take longer to answer than others. Don't rush – you should have plenty of time.

The questions won't try to trick you. If you're well prepared you won't find the questions difficult.

You'll be given 40 minutes to complete the test. If you have learning difficulties don't worry – you'll be given extra time.

When you've finished, look at the paper again and check your answers. If you're sure about your answers hand the paper in.

The result of your test will be sent to you within ten days.

The topics covered in the question paper

VEHICLE WEIGHTS AND DIMENSIONS

When driving a large vehicle you must be aware of

• **Vehicle size**	dimensions of your vehicle
• **Stowage and loading**	importance of a secure load
• **Excessive exhaust smoke**	the effect that dirty engines can have on the air around you
• **Vehicle markings**	clear markings required of vehicle size and dimensions

DRIVERS' HOURS AND REST PERIODS

Know the rules for the hours you work. You should have sound knowledge of

• **Driving limits**	EC driving limits and UK domestic hours rules
• **Keeping records**	what records to keep, how to keep them and what to do with them
• **Tachograph rules**	rules concerning the use of tachographs in the UK and abroad
• **Tiredness**	the reasons for not driving when tired
• **Vehicle security**	responsibility for your vehicle and load

BRAKING SYSTEMS AND SPEED LIMITERS

You should know the principle of how these work, including

- **Types of brake**   the different types of braking system used on vehicles

- **Maintenance and inspection**   the importance of ensuring that your brakes are in good working order

- **Proper use of the brakes**   when and how to use them

- **Tailgating**   understanding that following too closely can lead to harsh braking and accidents

- **Freezing conditions**   being aware of the effects of freezing weather on the braking system

CARRYING PASSENGERS

The safety and comfort of your passengers is very important. You should be aware of

- **Passenger comfort**   your passengers are paying customers and their safety and comfort are very important

- **Vehicle stability**   high and long vehicles must not be allowed to become unstable

- **Driver attitude**   a good attitude to passengers and other road users is important

- **Special passengers**   some passengers might have special needs

- **Safety equipment**   certain safety equipment must be carried on your vehicle. Other equipment is recommended for carriage

IN THE EVENT OF AN ACCIDENT

Your action at the scene of an accident could save lives. Your knowledge should include

- **Reducing risk**   good planning and anticipation. This will lessen the risk of an accident
- **Injuries**   what to do if someone is injured
- **Hazardous materials**   actions concerning other road users and reporting procedures
- **Casualties**   treatment and reporting procedures

VEHICLE CONDITION

Your vehicle must be in a good, safe condition. You should be responsible for

- **Safety checks**   checking brakes, steering and tyres. These are essential to ensure safe and legal driving
- **Legal requirements**   knowing what the law demands to ensure that your vehicle is in a safe and roadworthy condition

LEAVING THE VEHICLE

You should ensure that you and your passengers leave the vehicle safely. You must check

- **Mirrors and signals**   use your mirrors and give correct signals to ensure that other road users and passengers know your intentions
- **Passenger comfort**   choose the correct place to stop to help your passengers leave the vehicle safely
- **Driver's cab**   be aware of your own safety, and that of others, when you leave the vehicle's cab

VEHICLE LOADING

Your load or passengers must be carried safely. You should consider

- **Passenger safety**   your passengers' safety and comfort are your responsibility
- **Legal requirements**   be aware of the legal restrictions on your vehicle

RESTRICTED VIEW

You must use good all-round observation when driving a large vehicle.
To ensure this you should consider

- **Mirrors**   use your mirrors effectively to help spot hazards around you
- **Signals**   give clear and well-timed signals to help other road users understand your intentions
- **Parking**   understand that thoughtless parking might cause a hazard to both you and others on the road
- **Moving off**   practise good all-round observation to ensure safety
- **Blind spots**   understand that parts of your vehicle might restrict your vision. Extra effort should be taken to observe all round your vehicle
- **Observation at junctions**   practise good all-round observation to reduce the risk of an accident

OVERTAKING

To overtake safely you must always practise

- **Lane discipline**   use of the correct lane
- **Observation**   looking all round before overtaking

WINDY WEATHER

The wind can have an effect on the course of your vehicle. You should know about

- **High-sided vehicles** winds and high-sided vehicles together create a greater risk
- **Crosswinds** crosswinds are likely to be found on open, exposed roads
- **Air deflectors** there's equipment available to lessen wind resistance on your vehicle

HEAVY RAIN

Very heavy rain might affect the stability of your vehicle. Be aware of

- **Splashing spray** excessive spray from your vehicle will affect other road users
- **Saturated roads** the grip of your tyres is reduced on very wet roads

About Part Three

In this part you'll find the questions with the answers. They've been provided to help you to study for your theory test.

Most of the questions refer to drivers of *all* large vehicles. Specific questions for PCV drivers are marked with a bus symbol.

Questions for LGV drivers are marked with a lorry symbol.

Some of the questions in this book give 'correct' answers that don't apply to Northern Ireland. These are marked with an NI symbol and an explanation is given in the text.

DON'T JUST LEARN THE ANSWERS. It's important that you know *why* the answers are correct.

For easy reference and to help you study, the questions have been divided into topics and put into sections. Although this isn't how they'll be found in your question paper, it will be helpful if you want to refer to particular subjects.

In this book the questions are on the left-hand side of the page. Below each question you'll find the answers. Correct answers are in **bold** and are at the top of the list of options. This is for easy reference.

Please note that this isn't necessarily how you'll find them in your question paper.

On the right-hand side of the pages in this book there's a brief explanation of why the answer is correct. In addition, there will be some advice on correct driving procedures.

It's very important that you understand the reasons why the answers are correct. This will help you with your practical skills and help you to become a responsible professional driver.

If you find studying difficult or boring, try studying with friends. A question and answer session can be a good way of recalling facts later.

This section looks at rules on vehicle weights and dimensions.

The questions will ask you about

- Vehicle size

- Stowage and loading

- Excessive exhaust smoke

- Vehicle markings

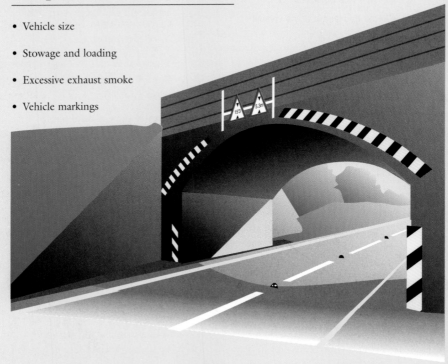

Question
A PCV driver should know the vehicle's unladen weight.
Where can this information be found?

Mark one answer

☒ On the side of the vehicle

☒ On the dashboard of the vehicle

☒ On the driver's duty roster

☒ On the depot noticeboard

Question
Maximum gross weight refers to the weight of

Mark one answer

☒ your vehicle with both luggage and passengers

☒ your vehicle with passengers but no luggage

☒ your vehicle without passengers or luggage

☒ your vehicle with luggage but no passengers

Question
Fifteen passengers on your vehicle would increase the weight by about

Mark one answer

☒ 1 tonne

☒ 0.5 tonnes

☒ 2.5 tonnes

☒ 3 tonnes

As a driver of a passenger carrying vehicle (PCV) you'll need to know about the

- weight (for restrictions)
- height (for clearances, etc.)
- width (for restrictions)
- length and ground clearance (for humpback bridges, grass verges, kerbs, etc.)

of your vehicle.

Weight limits are imposed on roads and bridges for two reasons

- the structure may not be capable of carrying greater loads
- to divert larger vehicles to more suitable routes

You're responsible for knowing the weight of your vehicle. Be aware of and understand the limits relating to any vehicle you drive. The unladen weight can be found on the side of your vehicle.

You must also be aware of the maximum gross weight (MGW), which refers to the weight of your vehicle with both passengers and luggage. This weight is also known as maximum authorised mass (MAM).

Fifteen passengers would add approximately 1 tonne to the weight of your vehicle. You should also allow for any luggage that they may be carrying.

Question
Certain weight limit signs don't apply to PCVs. How would the driver know?

Mark one answer

✖ **By a plate fitted beneath the weight limit sign**

✖ By the colour of the weight limit sign

✖ By a plate attached to the vehicle

✖ By a certificate carried by the driver

Question
What does this sign mean?

Mark one answer

✖ **Axle weight limit of 2 tonnes**

✖ No entry for two-axled trailers

✖ No entry for vehicles with two-speed axles

✖ Maximum gross weight of 2 tonnes

Some weight restrictions apply to large goods vehicles (LGVs) alone and not to passenger carrying vehicles (PCVs). Look out for a plate beneath a restriction sign that indicates this.

Road signs show weight restrictions in various ways and you should make yourself familiar with all of them so that you're in no doubt of their meaning and relevance.

Always look out for road signs, but you must be especially aware of those that refer to large or heavy vehicles. Get into the habit of checking for signs at junctions. There might be an indication on the junction layout sign. Before you turn ensure that you're using a road where there aren't any restrictions for the vehicle you're driving.

DSA THEORY TEST **for large vehicle drivers**

Question

What's the normal gross weight in the UK for an articulated LGV with five or more axles?

Mark one answer

- ☒ **38 tonnes**
- ☒ 36 tonnes
- ☒ 40 tonnes
- ☒ 45 tonnes

Question

Before driving over a level crossing you may need to telephone the signal operator if the total vehicle weight is over

Mark one answer

- ☒ **38 tonnes**
- ☒ 30 tonnes
- ☒ 32 tonnes
- ☒ 35 tonnes

The weight restrictions refer to the maximum gross weight (MGW), also known as maximum authorised mass (MAM). The normal MGW for articulated vehicles in the UK with five or more axles is 38 tonnes.

It's essential that you, the driver, ensure that the load is distributed correctly and safely either on or in your vehicle. Care should be taken to ensure that the front axle(s) of your vehicle isn't/aren't overloaded.

If you're driving a vehicle that's over 38 tonnes in weight you should plan your route very carefully. Try to avoid narrow roads, bridges and other places where the size and weight of your vehicle could cause delay to you or other road users.

If you have to drive over a level crossing there may be a danger of your vehicle grounding on the hump of the crossing. There might also be a risk of track damage from such a heavy, slow vehicle so you should use the telephone provided near the crossing to obtain permission to cross.

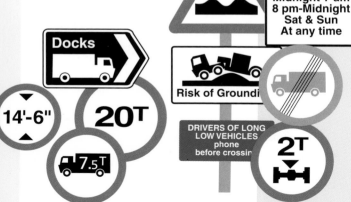

Question
What does this sign mean?

Safe height
16-6″

Mark one answer

☒ **Overhead electrical cable**

☒ Slippery road

☒ Double bend

☒ Cable laying ahead

Question
This sign means

Mark one answer

☒ **no vehicles over
14 feet 6 inches
high**

☒ no vehicles over
14 feet 6 inches
wide

☒ road humps
14 feet 6 inches
apart

☒ weight limit of
14.6 tonnes

Look out for restrictions that you may not have seen on a map. These may be temporary or, in the case of this sign, permanent.

You should also exercise care when entering

- loading bays
- bus and coach stations
- depots
- refuelling areas
- service station forecourts

or any premises that have

- overhanging canopies

Be careful when driving under

- bridges
- overhead cables
- overhead pipelines
- overhead walkways

or through road tunnels.

Always be aware of the height of the vehicle you're driving, especially if you drive a variety of types of vehicle or the loads you carry vary in shape or height.

Special maps are published that show weight and height limits on roads in the UK.

DSA THEORY TEST for large vehicle drivers

Question
Unless otherwise shown, the headroom under bridges in the UK is at least

Mark one answer

☒ **5.0 metres (16 feet 6 inches)**

☒ 5.5 metres (18 feet)

☒ 4.0 metres (13 feet)

☒ 4.1 metres (13 feet 4 inches)

Question
What's the minimum height of an unmarked bridge?

Mark one answer

☒ **5 metres (16 feet 6 inches)**

☒ 4.5 metres (15 feet)

☒ 4.7 metres (15 feet 6 inches)

☒ 4.8 metres (16 feet)

Every year there are more than 750 accidents where vehicles hit railway or motorway bridges, most involving buses, coaches and lorries. Don't let one of them be yours. Not only can it cause major disruption, but if you're carrying passengers it could kill or injure them. There are also the costs involved in making the bridge safe, re-aligning railway tracks and ensuring the safety of rail passengers.

If there isn't a minimum height shown on the bridge the headroom (in the UK) will be at least 5 metres (16 feet 6 inches).

If you hit a bridge, or see another vehicle hit a bridge, call Railtrack on 0345 003 355 and report the incident.

Question
What does this sign mean?

Mark one answer

✖ **No vehicles over 6 feet 6 inches wide**

☒ The width of the road is 6 feet 6 inches

☒ No vehicles over 6 feet 6 inches high

☒ Trailer length must not exceed 6 feet 6 inches

Question
What does this sign mean?

Mark one answer

✖ **No entry for vehicles over 32 feet 6 inches long**

☒ No entry for vehicles over 32.6 tonnes

☒ Warning of LGV straight ahead

☒ Warning of LGV crossing a one-way road

You must always be aware of the dimensions of your vehicle. Look out for road signs that show a width restriction. There will be an indication of this at the entrance to the road. Don't get into a situation where you have to reverse down a narrow road or alley because you haven't seen a sign.

You need to know the length of your vehicle as well as the height and width. Places where the length of your vehicle will be relevant are

• road tunnels
• level crossings
• ferries

DSA THEORY TEST for large vehicle drivers

Question
What does this sign mean?

Mark one answer

✖ **Risk of grounding**

☒ Humpbacked bridge

☒ Uneven road

☒ Road liable to subsidence

If you see this sign you must be alert to the danger of grounding. This can happen where there's a pronounced bump in the road, such as at a level crossing or a humpback bridge.

Question
You're driving a vehicle that's over 17 metres (55 feet) long.
What should you do at a level crossing?

Mark one answer

✖ **Stop before the crossing and phone the signal operator**

☒ Cross over using your horn and hazard warning lights

☒ Increase your speed to clear the crossing quickly

☒ Stop before the crossing, looking both ways before going on

If your vehicle is over 17 metres (55 feet) long and you wish to cross a level crossing you must stop before the level crossing and telephone the signal operator. There may be a risk of grounding as you drive your vehicle across.

Question
When a vehicle and load exceed a certain length the police must be notified and an attendant must be carried.
What's the length?

Mark one answer

☒ **27.4 metres (90 feet)**

☒ 15.5 metres (51 feet)

☒ 17 metres (55 feet)

☒ 18.7 metres (61 feet)

If your vehicle is over 27.4 metres (90 feet) in length you must notify the police before you undertake a journey. This length of vehicle is designed to be used to carry exceptionally long loads only. The vehicle will need an attendant and should be clearly marked with the appropriate boards to indicate its exceptional size.

Question
In which of the following places might vehicles over a certain length be restricted?

Mark three answers

☒ **In ferries**

☒ **In road tunnels**

☒ **On level crossings**

☒ In freight terminals

☒ On bridges

☒ On motorways

Look out for restrictions on long vehicles. There are few compared to width or height restrictions, but they're found where turning facilities are restricted or there's a risk of grounding, for example

- road tunnels
- level crossings
- ferries

DSA THEORY TEST for large vehicle drivers

Question

What types of fastenings or restraints should you use when carrying a heavy load of steel?

Mark one answer

☒ **Chains**

☒ Straps

☒ Ropes

☒ Sheeting

Question

Ideally, how should you secure a steel cargo container onto your vehicle or trailer? Using

Mark one answer

☒ **twist locks**

☒ battens and chocks

☒ straps

☒ ropes

YOU are responsible for the safety of the load you're carrying. At no time should the load endanger other road users. It's therefore vital that you ensure your load is secure and safely distributed on your vehicle. The method to ensure this will differ according to

- bulk
- weight
- the type of vehicle you're driving (flat bed, curtain side, etc.)
- the nature of the load

If you're carrying a heavy load such as steel, ropes or straps won't be strong enough to hold the strain when the vehicle is moving. In this case chains should be used, together with the compatible tensioning devices. These should be kept in good condition and used with the correct anchoring points.

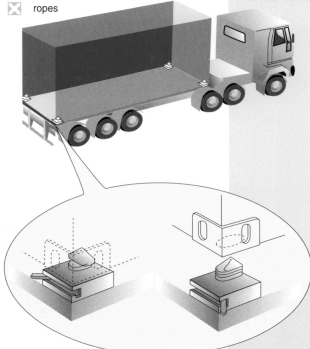

Question
How far can a load overhang at the rear
before you must use triangular projection
markers?

Mark one answer

 2 metres (6 feet 6 inches)

 1 metre (3 feet 4 inches)

 1.5 metres (5 feet)

2.9 metres (9 feet 6 inches)

It's not only important that you're aware of
the length of your vehicle, but other road
users should also be informed. This is to
enable them to understand the reason why
you might take up certain positions before
turning.

If the load on your vehicle overhangs by at
least 2 metres (6 feet 6 inches) it must have
marker boards.

Question
Long vehicle plates must be displayed on
vehicles longer than

Mark one answer

 13 metres (43 feet)

 10 metres (33 feet)

 11 metres (36 feet 3 inches)

 12 metres (39 feet 7 inches)

All vehicles that are over 13 metres (43 feet)
long must have Long Vehicle plates fitted to
the rear. These inform other road users and
will help them to judge how to deal with the
characteristics of your vehicle, such as when
they're overtaking or following your vehicle
as you're turning.

Question
How wide must a load be before you must
have triangular projection markers?

Mark one answer

 2.9 metres (9 feet 6 inches)

 2.6 metres (8 feet 6 inches)

2.7 metres (8 feet 10 inches)

 2.8 metres (9 feet 2 inches)

You must also ensure that any wide load is
shown by side markers. If your load is over
2.9 metres (9 feet 6 inches) wide then they
must be displayed. Make sure that they're
clearly visible, at both the front and rear,
and that they indicate the actual width
projection.

Question
Triangular projection markers are required
when your load is wider than 2.9 metres
(9 feet 6 inches).
What colour are these?

Mark one answer

 Red/white

 Black/yellow

 Red/yellow

Black/white

The marker boards should be red and white.
To ensure that they're seen clearly by other
road users they must be kept clean and
independently lit, especially during night
time and in bad visibility.

Question

Markings are required on the rear of LGVs over 7.5 tonnes maximum weight. What colour are these?

Mark one answer

☒ **Red/yellow**

☒ Red/white

☒ Black/yellow

☒ Black/white

All vehicles over 7.5 tonnes must have markings on the rear of the vehicle. These are to inform other road users of the different characteristics of your vehicle. These markings are rectangular and coloured red and yellow. They should be kept clean so that they're clearly visible at all times, including at night and in bad visibility.

Question

A passenger comments on exhaust smoke in the vehicle. You should

Mark one answer

☒ **stop and have the fault put right**

☒ report it as soon as you return to the depot

☒ avoid heavy revving of the engine when stationary

☒ have the emissions checked at the next vehicle inspection test

All road users should to try to reduce the effects that vehicles have on the environment. Larger vehicles have larger engines and therefore produce more exhaust fumes. Try to cut down on the amount of fumes that your vehicle produces, and don't increase them by

- revving the engine
- long static running
- ignoring comments about excessive smoke by passengers or other road users

This section looks at drivers' hours and rest periods.

The questions will ask you about

- EC and UK domestic driving limits
- Keeping records
- Tachograph rules
- Tiredness
- Vehicle security

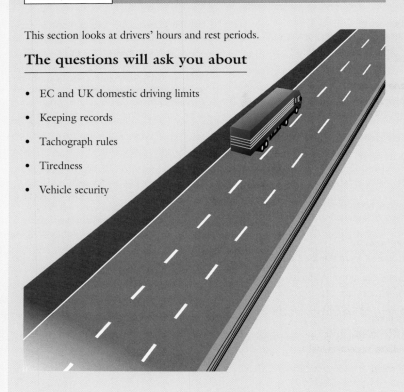

Question

You're on a regular service and aren't using a tachograph.
What MUST you carry with you?

Mark one answer

☒ **An extract from the duty roster and the service timetable**

☐ Tachograph charts from the previous seven days

☐ Your PCV driver's licence

☐ Servicing and maintenance records

Question

A PCV driver who isn't using a tachograph on a regular service of over 50 km (31 miles) must carry which TWO of these?

Mark two answers

☒ **An extract from the duty roster**

☒ **A copy of the service timetable**

☐ Some small change

☐ A detailed route map

☐ A drivers' hours record book

Whether you're driving an LGV or a PCV it's essential that you stay alert and are able to concentrate fully on your driving. There are rules to ensure that you don't drive for so long that you endanger the lives of other road users, your passengers or yourself.

Under EC rules, drivers' activities are usually recorded by means of a tachograph. This is an instrument in the cab that records information about the vehicle and driver.

However, if you're a PCV driver on a regular service over 50 km you may not be required to use one. Instead of using a tachograph you can carry an extract from the duty roster and a copy of the service timetable. The roster must show your name, the place where you're based and the schedule laid down in advance.

Question

What types of vehicle must be fitted with a tachograph when operating in the UK under EC rules?

Choose TWO of the following.

Mark two answers

☒ **Light goods vehicles drawing a trailer exceeding 3.5 tonnes gross weight**

☒ **Vehicles over 3.5 tonnes gross weight**

☒ Only vehicles between 3.5 and 7.5 tonnes gross weight

☒ Vehicles over 7.5 tonnes gross weight only used for driving instruction

☒ Vehicles manufactured before 1947

EC rules on drivers' hours and tachographs apply to drivers of most heavy goods where the maximum permissible gross weight limit (including any trailer) exceeds 3.5 tonnes. Domestic rules govern the remainder. You must be aware of which set of rules apply to the vehicle you're driving.

You'll be responsible if the information isn't recorded in the proper way.

Question

On an international journey in the EC when would a tachograph be needed?

If you have

Mark one answer

☒ **ten or more seats**

☒ less than ten seats

☒ less than eight seats

☒ eight or more seats

When undertaking an international journey within the EC you must use a tachograph if your vehicle has nine seats, including the driver's.

Question

The driver of a PCV with 18 seats on an excursion journey from London to Scotland should abide by which drivers' hours rules?

Mark one answer

☒ **EC only**

☒ AETR only

☒ Domestic

☒ EC and AETR

If you're driving a PCV on an excursion journey (that is, not a regular journey) and your vehicle has 18 or more seats you must use EC rules and record the details on a tachograph chart.

DSA THEORY TEST for large vehicle drivers

Question

A tachograph must be fitted to an LGV that's heavier than

Mark one answer

☒ **3.5 tonnes**

☒ 5 tonnes

☒ 7.5 tonnes

☒ 10 tonnes

Normally, a tachograph should be fitted and in full working order if your vehicle is over 3.5 tonnes. You should be aware of how it works and the regulations that refer to it.

Question

Who's responsible for the issue of tachograph charts to a PCV driver?

Mark one answer

☒ **The driver's employer**

☒ The Department of Transport

☒ The authorised calibration centre

☒ The local MOT testing station

Your employer is responsible for the issue of tachograph charts. You, the driver, must ensure that the correct information is recorded on the tachograph chart.

Question

Before starting driving which of the following should you complete on the centre field of your tachograph chart?

Mark one answer

☒ **The place from which you start your day's journey**

☒ Details of the goods carried

☒ The name and address of your employer

☒ The amount of daily rest taken prior to starting the shift

Before departing on your journey you must record on the tachograph chart the date and the place where the use of the chart begins.

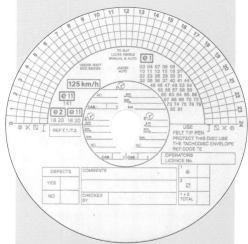

Question

You must have enough tachograph charts with you for your journey.
You'll need at least one for every

Mark one answer

☒ **24 hours**

☒ 10 hours

☒ 36 hours

☒ 48 hours

Question

You're driving a vehicle requiring the use of a tachograph. You must carry charts for the current week and the last

Mark one answer

☒ **day of the previous week on which you drove**

☒ seven days on which you drove

☒ 14 days on which you drove

☒ 28 days on which you drove

Your employer should supply you with enough tachograph charts for the entire journey. You'll need at least one for every 24 hours.

Department of Transport (DOT) enforcement staff and the police have powers to inspect drivers' hours and other documents. In Northern Ireland the inspections are carried out by the Department of the Environment for Northern Ireland (DOENI).

The obligation to make sure that all records are completed correctly falls on you, the driver, as well as the operator. There are heavy fines imposed for the misuse or falsification of charts.

DSA THEORY TEST for large vehicle drivers

Question

Within how many days must drivers return completed tachograph charts to their employer?

Mark one answer

☒ **21 days**

☒ 25 days

☒ 30 days

☒ 35 days

Question

During your working day you're changing to another vehicle with the same type of tachograph. What should you do with your tachograph chart?

Mark one answer

☒ **Take the chart with you and use it in the other vehicle**

☒ Use the chart that's already in the other vehicle

☒ Record your driving hours in a record book

☒ Install a new chart in the other vehicle

An enforcement officer is entitled to inspect and copy any tachograph chart. The officer can detain a vehicle for inspection and, if a false record is suspected, the chart may be taken and kept for up to six months. The officer will issue you with a receipt or write their name and telephone number on the back of the replacement chart.

To ensure that all records are kept up to date and available for inspection by enforcement staff you must give the completed charts to your employer within 21 days.

If you're changing vehicles during the working day you should take your chart with you and use it in the next vehicle. This isn't always possible, however, as charts produced by different manufacturers may not fit each other's equipment. In this case you should use another chart, ensuring that all the information for the day is recorded.

Question
The tachograph on your vehicle becomes faulty.
It can be repaired on return to base if this is within

Mark one answer
☒ **one week**
☒ 18 hours
☒ 56 hours
☒ two weeks

If the tachograph on your vehicle becomes faulty you should take it to an approved tachograph repairer as soon as possible. If your vehicle can't return to your base within a week of discovery of its defective operation the repair must be carried out while you're away on the journey. While the tachograph is faulty or broken you must keep a manual record of your activities on a temporary chart.

Question
Your tachograph chart becomes dirty or damaged.
What should you do?

Mark one answer
☒ **Use a spare chart and attach it to the damaged one**
☒ Continue with the same chart and enter the details in writing
☒ Use a spare chart and destroy the damaged chart
☒ Continue to use the chart

If your current tachograph chart becomes damaged you should start another and then attach it to the damaged one. Your records must be clear and up to date at all times.

It's sensible to carry spare tachograph charts, that is, more than you think you'll need for your journey. You'll be able to use a spare one if your chart becomes dirty or damaged.

Question
During your break your vehicle will be moved by another person.
What should you do with the tachograph chart?

Mark one answer
☒ **Remove the chart and make a manual record of the break period**
☒ Leave the chart in the vehicle and record the changes on the back
☒ Put in a new chart on your return to the vehicle
☒ Switch to rest mode to record the break

If your vehicle is likely to be used by another person while you're away from it you should take your tachograph chart with you. Your break from driving should be entered on the reverse of the chart.

DSA THEORY TEST for large vehicle drivers

Question

Under EC rules a driver must take a break after a continuous driving period of

Mark one answer

✖ 4.5 hours

✖ 3 hours

✖ 4 hours

✖ 5.5 hours

Question

You've been driving an LGV without a break for four and a half hours. Under EC rules a break must be taken.
How long must it be?

Mark one answer

✖ 45 minutes

✖ 30 minutes

✖ 35 minutes

✖ 40 minutes

Question

EC rules require that after driving continuously for the maximum period a PCV driver must take a break.
This must be at least

Mark one answer

✖ 45 minutes

✖ 15 minutes

✖ 30 minutes

✖ 60 minutes

Whether you're driving an LGV or a PCV it's essential that you don't become over-tired by driving for excessively long periods of time. EC rules are in place to prevent this happening. You must follow these rules and ensure that the details of your journey are recorded. These details must be available for inspection by DOT or DOENI enforcement staff. For this reason you should make sure that you know the rules relating to the vehicle you're driving and the journey you're making.

If you're driving under EC rules you must not drive continuously for more than 4.5 hours without taking a break. If you've driven continually for four and a half hours you must take a break of at least 45 minutes. Include your stops in the timetable when you're planning your journey.

Always park your vehicle in a safe place off the road. Try to find a place where you can get out of your vehicle for refreshment. This will help to ensure that you're fully refreshed.

If you're carrying passengers they'll also be grateful for a break. Taking breaks at the correct time will ensure that your passengers are safe and comfortable.

Question

Under EC rules the break needed after a maximum period of driving may be replaced by several shorter breaks taken during the driving period.

Each shorter break must be at least

Mark one answer

- ☒ **15 minutes**
- ☒ 20 minutes
- ☒ 30 minutes
- ☒ 45 minutes

A 45-minute continuous break can be replaced by several shorter breaks during the 4.5 hours driving period. These breaks must be at least 15 minutes.

Question

Under EC rules you can drive for a maximum of nine hours daily.

How many days of the week can this be extended to ten hours?

Mark one answer

- ☒ **Two**
- ☒ One
- ☒ Three
- ☒ Four

Under EC rules your normal daily driving must not exceed nine hours. This nine hours must be the time between

- any two daily rest periods
- a daily rest period and a weekly rest period

It's permitted to extend these hours to ten hours twice a week.

A 'day' is generally any 24-hour period beginning with the resumption of other work or driving after the last daily or weekly rest period.

Question

Under EC rules what's the maximum daily driving time allowed?

Mark one answer

- ☒ **Nine hours extended to ten hours on two days of the week**
- ☒ Nine hours extended to 11 hours on three days of the week
- ☒ Ten hours extended to 11 hours on two days of the week
- ☒ Ten hours extended to 11 hours on three days of the week

Question

Under EC rules you may drive for a maximum of nine hours daily.
On two days of the week this may be increased to

Mark one answer

☒ **10 hours**

☐ 9.5 hours

☐ 11 hours

☐ 11.5 hours

Don't drive for more than the maximum hours allowed. You're permitted to extend the daily nine hours to ten hours twice a week.

Question

Under EC rules your minimum daily rest is 11 hours.
On three days of the week this may be reduced to

Mark one answer

☒ **nine hours**

☐ seven hours

☐ eight hours

☐ ten hours

Under EC rules you must have a minimum daily rest of 11 consecutive hours. This may be reduced to nine hours on not more than three days a week, as long as the reduction is compensated by an equivalent rest before the end of the following week.

Question

Under EC rules what's the normal weekly rest that must be taken?

Mark one answer

☒ **45 hours**

☐ 40 hours

☐ 41 hours

☐ 42 hours

Working weeks are defined as periods between 00.00 hours on Monday and 24.00 hours on the following Sunday. When taking the weekly rest period, a daily rest period must normally be extended to at least 45 consecutive hours.

Question

Which one of the following symbols on your tachograph indicates your break/rest period?

Mark one answer

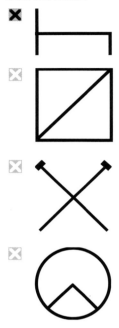

A tachograph is fitted with a mode switch, which allows you to select the task that you're undertaking. When the mode has been selected the time spent on that particular activity is then recorded onto the chart automatically.

Each activity has a different symbol. You should know what each symbol means so that your records are correct.

- Driving symbol

- Other work symbol

- On duty and available for work

- Break or rest symbol

DSA THEORY TEST for large vehicle drivers

Question

What does this tachograph chart symbol mean?

Mark one answer

 Driving

 Driver at rest

 Chart not required

Other work

Each activity has a different symbol on a tachograph chart. You should know what the different symbols mean so that you can select the correct one. You'll be responsible if you fail to record all your activities correctly.

Some new tachographs don't have a 'driving' mode switch. This is because these tachographs will automatically record driving time on the chart whenever the vehicle is moved, no matter what mode the switch is turned to.

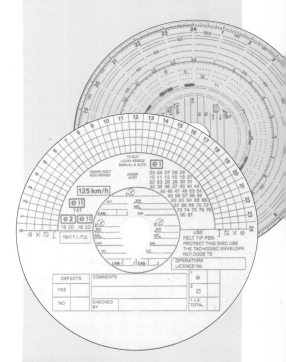

Question

You're driving a vehicle with a tachograph. What does this symbol mean?

Mark one answer

✖ **Driver doing other work**

▢ Driving period

▢ Rest period

▢ Working under domestic rules

If you're working away from the vehicle and can't leave your tachograph chart in, you should take the chart with you and make a manual entry on the reverse side, for example

OW (other work) 09.15–10.00

Question

Under EC rules what's the maximum number of days that you can drive in a week?

Mark one answer

✖ **Six**

▢ Four

▢ Five

▢ Seven

You're only allowed to drive up to six days of the week.

Question

Under EC rules what's the maximum driving time allowed in a fortnight?

Mark one answer

✖ **90 hours**

▢ 85 hours

▢ 100 hours

▢ 105 hours

The maximum number of hours that you can drive in a fortnight is 90 hours. These hours don't have to be split evenly, but the total number of hours spent driving in any one week shouldn't exceed 56 hours.

Don't exceed your driving hours. You'll need to keep records of how many hours you drive in a day, a week and a fortnight. Learn the rules and adhere to them. Heavy fines can be imposed for failure to do so.

Question
At the end of your working week you've driven a total of 56 hours.
What's the maximum number of hours that you can drive in the following week under EC rules?

Mark one answer

☒ **34**

☒ 36

☒ 38

☒ 40

If you've driven a total of 56 hours in any one week you can only drive for 34 hours in the following week.

If your hours add up to a total of 56 in any one week you must make sure that you don't exceed the permitted hours the following week. Keep your own record to make sure that you don't exceed these hours.

Question
A driver's daily rest period may be taken in a parked vehicle if

Mark one answer

☒ **it's fitted with a bunk**

☒ there's a smoke alarm fitted

☒ the vehicle is in an authorised coach park

☒ there are no passengers on the vehicle

Question
Under EC rules you may interrupt daily rest periods. When?

Mark one answer

☒ **If part of it's taken on board a ferry or train**

☒ When loading or unloading the vehicle

☒ When there isn't more than a one-hour gap between rest periods

☒ When your journey includes night driving

Some vehicles are fitted with sleeping accommodation for the driver. If your vehicle is fitted with this facility you're permitted to take your daily rest period there, provided your vehicle is stationary.

If you're covering part of your journey by boat or train the following rules apply

- the daily rest period may be interrupted but only once, and if it is, two hours must be added to the total rest time

- if the rest period is interrupted, one part must be taken on land, either before or after the journey. The other part can be taken on the boat or train

- any interruption in rest must be as short as possible and no more than one hour before or after getting off the boat or train, including any Customs checks.

- during both parts of the rest period the driver(s) must have access to a bunk or couchette

- time spent on a ferry boat or train that isn't treated as daily rest can be treated as a break

Question

Which TWO of the following are most likely to cause tiredness?

Mark two answers

☒ **Insufficient breaks from driving**

☒ **The driving area becoming too warm**

☒ The driving area becoming too cool

☒ Driving breaks taken on board the vehicle

☒ Modern vehicles with air suspension

☒ Modern vehicles with quieter rear-mounted engines

Question

When driving, you start to feel tired or unable to concentrate.
You should

Mark one answer

☒ **stop as soon as it's safe to do so**

☒ wind down a window and carry on

☒ switch on the radio to help you to concentrate

☒ speed up to get to your destination sooner

Tiredness will affect your concentration. It's most important that you don't allow yourself to become weary by not taking proper breaks or rest periods. As a professional driver you have a responsibility for either goods or passengers, as well as overall road safety.

Try to ensure that your vehicle is well ventilated. Open a window or turn down the heating to prevent yourself becoming drowsy.

If you start to feel tired you should stop as soon as it's safe to do so, even if you aren't due a break.

Make sure that you get enough sleep the night before you're due to work, especially if you're on an early shift.

Question

You feel tired after 2.5 hours' driving.
What should you do?

Mark one answer

✖ **Stop as soon as it's safe to do so**

✖ Slow down to a safer speed

✖ Reduce your planned driving time to
3.5 hours

✖ Take a less busy route

Most accidents happen as a result of a lapse of concentration. Don't let this happen to you. If you start to feel tired you won't perform as well as you should. Your anticipation will slow down and your judgement of hazards will become flawed. It will be better for you, and the safety of other road users, if you stop and rest as soon as it's safe to do so.

Question

You're driving on a motorway and suddenly become tired.
What should you do?

Mark one answer

✖ **Leave by the next exit and find a
place to stop**

✖ Stop on the hard shoulder and rest

✖ Stop on the next slip road and rest

✖ Stop on the verge off the motorway
and rest

If you're driving for long distances on a motorway take plenty of rest stops. There have been many accidents blamed on drivers falling asleep at the wheel. If you feel yourself becoming 'mesmerised' stop at the next service area.

Question

You're feeling tired when driving on a motorway.
Where can you stop?

Mark one answer

✖ **At a service station**

✖ On the hard shoulder

✖ On a slip road

✖ In a deceleration lane

Travelling long distances on a motorway can have a 'mesmerising' effect. Any lack of concentration, however brief, could lead to an accident. Stop as soon as you can, however don't stop on the hard shoulder. Leave the motorway by the next exit and pull over in a safe place to rest. Ideally you should use a service area, where you can have a rest and refreshment before you restart your journey.

Question
You're driving an LGV at night.
What can you do to help you keep alert?

Mark three answers

☒ **Keep plenty of cool fresh air moving through the cab**

☒ **Take proper rest periods at correct intervals**

☒ **Walk around in fresh air after a rest stop**

☐ Eat a heavy meal before setting off

☐ Keep the cab warm and comfortable

☐ Drive faster to get to your destination sooner

Driving at night can make you feel tired more quickly. If you're starting your shift at the end of the day make sure that you have enough rest before you start work. You must be able to stay alert for the duration of your shift.

Make sure that you have good ventilation in the cab. This will help you to stay alert by making sure that there's enough fresh air. Stale, warm air will dull your senses and cause drowsiness.

Question
You're driving an LGV on a motorway and you're getting drowsy. There are no service areas or exits for some distance.
What should you do?

Mark one answer

☒ **Open the window and turn the heating down**

☐ Stop on the hard shoulder and rest

☐ Slow down and use the hazard warning lights

☐ Increase your speed to get to the next service area sooner

During very cold weather it's tempting to have the heating in the cab fully turned on. Try to stay aware of the effect this could have on your reactions and anticipation. It could dull them by making you feel drowsy and tired.

Question
You're driving an LGV. During the journey you're feeling ill and unable to concentrate.
What should you do?

Mark one answer

☒ **Stop in a safe place and seek help**

☐ Continue your journey and keep your windows open

☐ Increase your speed to finish your work earlier

☐ Keep stopping at regular intervals for rest

If you become unwell it will affect your concentration. You must be fully alert and ready for any hazards that might occur while you drive. Stop in a safe place and seek assistance. You may have to call out a relief driver to complete the journey for you.

DSA THEORY TEST for large vehicle drivers

Question

What should you do if asked to leave your PCV by an official who isn't in uniform?

Mark one answer

✖ **Request to see a warrant card**

☒ Comply with the request

☒ Refuse to leave the vehicle

☒ Invite the official aboard

If you're requested to leave your vehicle by an official who's not in uniform ask to see their warrant card. The official is likely to be a DOT or DOENI enforcement officer or a police officer, but don't presume this.

Question

When a PCV is left unattended the driver MUST ensure that

Mark one answer

✖ **the parking brake is applied**

☒ the tachograph sheet is removed

☒ the gear lever is in neutral

☒ the gear lever is in either first or reverse gear

Always ensure that your vehicle is safe when you leave it unattended. Always apply the parking brake. Don't just leave it in gear.

This section looks at braking systems and speed limiters.

The questions will ask you about

- Types of brake

- Maintenance and inspection

- Proper use of the brakes

- Tailgating

- Freezing conditions

Question

On a three-line braking system to the trailer of an LGV what colour is the auxiliary line?

Mark one answer

☒ **Blue**

☒ Red

☒ Green

☒ Yellow

Question

What could prevent air pressure building up in an air brake system in cold frosty weather?

Mark one answer

☒ **Moisture drawn in with the air may freeze and cause a blockage**

☒ Moisture in the air may form bubbles in the brake fluid

☒ The air will contract, reducing the pressure

☒ The dampness may cause valves to rust

If you're driving an articulated vehicle or a trailer combination it's vital that you understand the rules that apply to coupling and uncoupling the brake lines. If you're taking a test with a trailer you'll be expected to demonstrate this during your practical test. The lines must be connected strictly in accordance with the correct procedure. Study the information in *The Goods Vehicle Driving Manual* to ensure that you know and understand the way this should be done.

Large vehicles normally have braking systems that use compressed air to control the action of the brake shoes. The compressed air is built up by the vehicle's engine and stored in tanks on the chassis. This compressed air is therefore vital to the effectiveness of the brakes. You must understand the system and know how to keep it in good condition so that the brakes won't fail when you need them.

Question

What could prevent the buildup of brake air pressure on a PCV in frosty weather?

When the weather is frosty any moisture in the storage tanks may freeze and prevent pressure building up properly.

Mark one answer

☒ **Moisture freezing in the system**

☒ Lack of antifreeze in storage tanks

☒ Insufficient lagging of tanks and pipes

☒ Low engine revolutions

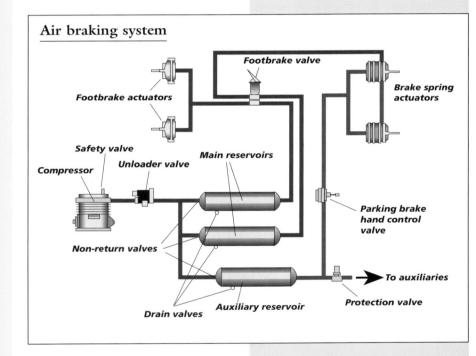

Air braking system

Footbrake valve

Footbrake actuators

Brake spring actuators

Safety valve

Compressor

Unloader valve

Main reservoirs

Parking brake hand control valve

Non-return valves

To auxiliaries

Drain valves

Auxiliary reservoir

Protection valve

DSA THEORY TEST for large vehicle drivers

Question

In frosty weather, what precaution could an LGV driver take to prevent moisture freezing in brake air storage tanks?

Mark one answer

☒ **Drain the tanks daily**

☐ Cover the tanks with a blanket

☐ Keep the engine at high revs when starting

☐ Pump the brakes

Question

What action would you take if a brake pressure warning device comes on?

Mark one answer

☒ **Stop and get the fault put right**

☐ Continue to drive the vehicle

☐ Drain the air tanks

☐ Disconnect all the air lines

You should make sure that you drain the tanks daily and add some antifreeze to the system to avoid moisture freezing. Most modern vehicles have an automatic draining system. These should be checked regularly.

Air brake systems are fitted with a warning device that sounds if the air pressure in the tanks drops below a safe level. This may be a warning buzzer and/or pressure gauges. You must always be aware of the function of all gauges on your vehicle and check them as you drive.

If the warning light indicating a loss of brake pressure comes on then you must stop and get the fault put right immediately. The safety of your load or, even more importantly, your passengers will be at risk.

Question
An anti-lock braking system is designed to

Mark one answer

☒ prevent the wheels from locking up under braking

☒ prevent an articulated vehicle from jack-knifing

☒ prevent the driving wheels from spinning

☒ prevent moisture from building up inside the braking system

Question
An anti-lock braking system will operate on an LGV when

Mark one answer

☒ the wheels are about to lock under braking

☒ driving on an icy road

☒ driving too fast around a bend

☒ progressive braking is required

Question
The correct procedure for stopping an LGV equipped with an anti-lock braking system in an emergency is to

Mark one answer

☒ apply the footbrake firmly in one application until the vehicle has stopped

☒ apply the footbrake firmly in a pumping action until the vehicle has stopped

☒ apply the footbrake and handbrake until the vehicle has stopped

☒ apply the handbrake only

Anti-lock braking systems are required by law on certain large goods vehicles and trailer combinations. The term ABS (anti-lock braking system) is the registered trade mark of Bosch (Germany) for Anti Blockiersystem.

An ABS system uses sensors to detect the moment when the wheels are about to lock. Just before the wheels lock, the system reduces the braking and then re-applies it. This action may happen many times a second to maintain braking performance.

If you're driving a vehicle with anti-lock brakes and you feel the vehicle beginning to skid you should keep your foot firmly on the brake pedal until the vehicle stops. This will allow the system to work.

Although an ABS on a vehicle makes a contribution to safe braking it doesn't take away the need to drive with good planning and anticipation, which will greatly reduce the need to brake harshly. Reliable and efficient equipment is essential but it's your action that could prevent an accident.

Question

An anti-lock braking system warning light fitted to a PCV should go out

Mark one answer

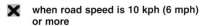

✗   when road speed is 10 kph (6 mph) or more

✗   when the brakes are used for the first time

✗   immediately after the anti-lock braking system comes into operation

✗   when the secondary braking system is used

Question

What fault could be indicated if 'pumping' of the footbrake pedal is necessary before hydraulic brakes operate?

Mark one answer

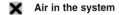

✗   Air in the system

✗   Leak in the system

✗   Worn brake pads

✗   Overheated brake drums

Question

What is 'brake fade'?

Mark one answer

✗   Reduction of braking effectiveness

✗   Reduction of air pressure

✗   Smooth progressive braking

✗   Low hydraulic brake fluid level

Every vehicle fitted with an ABS must have a warning light fitted in the cab of the vehicle. Check this as part of your routine. Make yourself fully familiar with the warnings and gauges if you're driving the vehicle for the first time. Driving with a defective ABS may constitute an offence.

Warning lamps may differ between manufacturers but the warning light should come on with the ignition. The light should go out when the vehicle reaches 10 kph (6 mph). Don't carry on any further if the light fails to go out. The safety of your passengers and all other road users will be at risk.

A hydraulic braking system uses the flow of oil compressed in pipes to operate the brake shoes or pads. If the vehicle you're driving uses this system and you feel the need to 'pump' the brake pedal, there could be air in the pipes. Report this immediately. Any fault in a braking system will put you and other road users at risk.

Make sure that you're in the correct gear before you negotiate downhill stretches of road. A low gear will assist with the braking and prevent the vehicle gaining momentum as it negotiates the hill. Look out for road signs. Look well ahead for a 'dead road', which would indicate a dip or a hill.

Continually using the brakes, for example on downhill stretches, could cause the brakes to 'fade'. This will mean that your brakes are less effective.

Question
What would cause the brakes to 'fade'?

Mark one answer

☒ Continuous use of the brakes

☒ Contaminated brake linings

☒ Moisture in the storage tanks

☒ Brakes out of adjustment

Question
To help to avoid 'brake fade' LGV drivers should ensure that

Mark one answer

☒ the appropriate gears are engaged before downhill gradients

☒ the air tanks are drained before journeys

☒ air pressure is correct

☒ the handbrake is applied before stopping

Question
'Brake fade' is a loss of effectiveness of the brakes, caused by their continuous use. When would this be most likely to happen?

Mark one answer

☒ On a long downhill gradient

☒ On a long journey

☒ When approaching hazards

☒ On a long uphill gradient

It's important that you don't continually use the brakes. The brake shoes and drum can become hot from over-use. If this happens the drum will expand and move away from the shoes. Also, the friction material on the brake shoes can be affected by the heat generated. It can become shiny and therefore ineffective and slippery against the drum. This is often referred to as 'brake fade'.

When you're driving a large vehicle downhill the effects of gravity will tend to make the vehicle's speed increase. This will result in more braking effort and an increase in the stopping distance.

It's important that you engage a low gear as you approach the hill to ensure the engine is building up air and can assist with braking.

If the road has a long downhill gradient this is very important. You should be anticipating hazards like this as you drive. Always be in the correct gear for the situation. Good planning and preparation will ensure that you are.

Continuous use of the brakes will cause them to overheat. In extreme cases the brakes will fail to work. When you're going downhill the weight of your vehicle will push down and increase the momentum so you'll gather speed very quickly. Don't underestimate the importance of the correct use of your brakes.

DSA THEORY TEST for large vehicle drivers

Question
What causes 'brake fade'?

Mark one answer

☒ **Continuous use of the brakes**

☒ Repeated pumping of the brakes

☒ Loss of air pressure in the system

☒ Badly worn brake pads

Question
What is the cause of 'brake fade'?

Mark one answer

☒ **Continuous use of the brakes**

☒ Poorly adjusted clutch

☒ Service brake in operation

☒ Badly worn brake shoes or discs

Question
Exhaust brakes give greatest efficiency when used

Mark one answer

☒ **at high engine speed in low gears**

☒ at low engine speed in high gears

☒ on stop–start town work

☒ on high-speed motorway runs

The continuous use of the brakes on a long downhill gradient can cause them to overheat. This could result in loss of braking control.

You should engage a low gear to enable the engine to assist with the braking. This will also ensure that there's enough air pressure building up in the tanks.

Because excessive braking can have serious effects on the brakes some vehicles are fitted with exhaust brakes. These brakes can alter the engine's exhaust flow, using it to assist with the braking. They're most efficient when the engine is at high speed and in a low gear, such as when descending a long hill. Using the exhaust brakes can relieve the service brakes, preventing them from becoming hot and failing through over-use.

Question

You're descending a long hill and want to avoid the brakes overheating.
The vehicle's speed should be stabilised by using the

Mark one answer

❌ **endurance brake (retarder)**

☒ anti-lock braking system

☒ footbrake

☒ secondary brake

Question

A system for controlling the vehicle's speed without using the wheel brakes is

Mark one answer

❌ **an endurance brake (retarder)**

☒ a secondary brake

☒ a differential lock

☒ an emergency air system

Question

An endurance brake (retarder) may work by which TWO of the following ways?

Mark two answers

❌ **Increasing engine braking**

❌ **Using an extra transmission device**

☒ Sensing wheel speed

☒ Using the parking brake

☒ Using the secondary brake

Systems that assist in controlling a vehicle's speed without using the wheel brakes are called endurance brakes or 'retarders'. Retarders operate by applying resistance via the transmission to the rotation of the vehicle's driven wheels. This may be achieved by

- increased engine braking
- exhaust braking
- transmission-mounted electromagnetic or hydraulic devices

If your vehicle is fitted with any of these devices you must become familiar with them before you make your journey. You won't lose respect by asking a colleague to show you, but you will if you have an accident through ignorance.

Question
The MOST powerful brake on a PCV is normally the

Mark one answer

❌ **service brake**

⬜ secondary brake

⬜ anti-lock braking system

⬜ endurance brake (retarder)

The most powerful and effective brakes on the vehicle are the service brakes and these should be used in normal circumstances. Well-maintained brakes should apply an even pressure to all the wheels, providing an efficient controlled stop.

Question
The service brake on a PCV operates on

Mark one answer

❌ **all wheels**

⬜ drive wheels on the rear

⬜ steering wheels

⬜ the same wheels as the parking brake

The service brake operates on all wheels, allowing an even application and controlled stop.

Question
When making a short stop, facing uphill, you should

Mark one answer

❌ **apply the handbrake after stopping**

⬜ hold the vehicle on the clutch

⬜ hold the vehicle on the footbrake

⬜ select neutral and apply the handbrake

If you have to make a stop on an uphill gradient wait until the vehicle has come to a stop before applying the handbrake, just as you would normally.

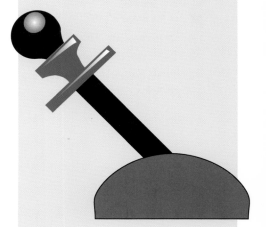

Question
Which THREE of the following are advantages
of progressive braking when driving a PCV?

Mark three answers

☒ **Passenger safety and comfort**

☒ **Lower fuel consumption**

☒ **Reduced tyre wear**

☒ Increased air brake pressure

☒ 'Brake fade' is avoided

As a driver of a PCV the safety and comfort
of your passengers is the first priority. If you
have the correct attitude when you're
driving, your passengers will be assured of a
comfortable and pleasant journey. By good
forward planning and anticipation you'll be
able to prevent harsh braking and late sharp
steering. These factors will also have a
bearing on the maintenance and condition
of your vehicle. Badly driven vehicles cost
more to run and maintain.

Question
You're the driver of a 1996 PCV, which must
be fitted with a speed limiter.
At what speed is the limiter set?

Mark one answer

☒ **62 mph (100 kph)**

☒ 60 mph (96 kph)

☒ 70 mph (112 kph)

☒ 75 mph (120 kph)

A speed limiter must prevent the vehicle
from exceeding a set limit.

Question
When a speed limiter is fitted to a PCV where
must the setting be displayed clearly?

Mark one answer

☒ **In the driver's cab**

☒ On the nearside of the vehicle

☒ On the rear of the vehicle

☒ On the driver's side at the front of the
vehicle

If there's a limiter fitted to the vehicle there
should be a notice clearly displayed in the
driver's cab showing the speed at which
it's set.

Question
What's the national speed limit for an LGV over 7.5 tonnes on a motorway?

Mark one answer

X **60 mph (96 kph)**

☒ 50 mph (80 kph)

☒ 55 mph (88 kph)

☒ 70 mph (112 kph)

Question
At 50 mph (80 kph) what gap should an LGV driver leave behind the vehicle in front on a dry, level road?

Mark one answer

X **Two-second gap minimum**

☒ One vehicle length

☒ 18 metres (60 feet) minimum

☒ Five car lengths

Question
You're behind a large vehicle. How can you improve your view ahead?

Mark one answer

X **Stay further back**

☒ Move over to the right

☒ Move over to the left

☒ Overtake as soon as you can

Be aware of and obey all speed limits. Think about this when you're considering overtaking. On a motorway an LGV's speed shouldn't exceed 60 mph.

'Tailgating' is a common and very dangerous practice. It often happens on motorways and occurs when one vehicle travels too close to another vehicle in front of it. Don't do it.

Tailgating is often the cause of serious accidents. It's essential that you understand the distance it will take for you to stop if you have do so in an emergency. Always leave a safety margin.

Leaving a safety margin will improve your view of the road ahead. Staying back from the vehicle in front will allow you more room to react to hazards that might occur. If you're thinking about overtaking, staying back will allow you to see more of the road ahead. Don't take risks.

A good way to check whether you're too close to another vehicle is by using the two-second rule. Pick an object some distance ahead, for example a bridge, sign or lamp-post. As the vehicle in front passes it, begin to say

'Only a fool breaks the two-second rule.'

If you pass the object before you've finished saying it YOU'RE TOO CLOSE. Drop back and try the test again.

Question

You're driving an LGV at a speed of 50 mph (80 kph) in good, dry conditions.
What distance should you stay behind the vehicle in front?

Mark one answer

✗ **At least 50 metres (164 feet)**

✗ At least 20 metres (66 feet)

✗ At least 30 metres (98 feet)

✗ At least 40 metres (131 feet)

You should always leave a safety margin between you and the vehicle in front. This gap will give you a better view of the road ahead. It will also allow you more time to react if the traffic in front changes speed or direction.

Question

At 50 mph (80 kph) what gap should an LGV driver leave from the vehicle in front on a wet, level road?

Mark one answer

✗ **Four-second gap minimum**

✗ One vehicle length

✗ 37 metres (120 feet) minimum

✗ Ten car lengths

You must be aware of the fact that wet roads can increase stopping distance to at least double that required on dry roads. You'll have to count four seconds instead of two, so say the phrase twice.

You should always drive in accordance with the conditions. If the weather changes for the worse you should adjust your driving accordingly.

Question

When driving in snow, stopping distances may be increased by up to how much compared with a dry road?

Mark one answer

✗ **Ten times**

✗ Two times

✗ Five times

✗ One vehicle length

In icy or snowy weather your stopping distance can increase by up to ten times. Because snowy weather increases the distance needed to stop you must look well ahead and leave a good safety margin. It's easy to underestimate the different stopping distances needed in bad weather. You should be aware that ten times the normal stopping distance is a long way.

Question

When required to slow down or stop on an icy road LGV drivers should make sure that

Mark one answer

☒ **braking is gentle and in good time**

☒ retarders are always used

☒ downward gear changes are made

☒ the handbrake is used in a rapid on-and-off movement

When you have to slow down or stop you should avoid harsh, late braking. If you're planning ahead with good anticipation you can reduce the need to brake harshly. Brake gently and in good time to ensure control of your vehicle. This is particularly important on icy or slippery roads.

Question

While driving on a very wet road with surface water your vehicle starts to aquaplane. You should take your foot off the accelerator and

Mark one answer

☒ **not apply the brakes**

☒ apply the footbrake firmly

☒ apply the footbrake with a pumping action

☒ apply the handbrake gently

If you feel the vehicle start to aquaplane don't apply the brakes. This will cause the wheels to lift further off the road's surface and make the situation worse. Look ahead and try to be ready for situations where the road surface could have an effect on your control of the vehicle.

If your vehicle is fitted with an ABS make sure that you know what the manufacturer recommends in these circumstances.

Question

After driving through a flood what should an LGV driver do?

Mark one answer

☒ **Drive in low gear with the footbrake lightly applied**

☒ Carry out an emergency stop

☒ Avoid braking until the brakes are dried out

☒ Pump the footbrake when approaching hazards

If you have to drive through a flood do so with caution. Ensure that the brakes on your vehicle haven't been impaired by the deep water. Once out of the flood drive in a low gear with the brakes gently applied. Don't forget to consider what's behind you before doing so.

SECTION 4 CARRYING PASSENGERS

This section looks at the rules concerning carrying passengers.

The questions will ask you about

- Passenger comfort

- Vehicle stability

- Driver attitude

- Special passengers

- Safety equipment

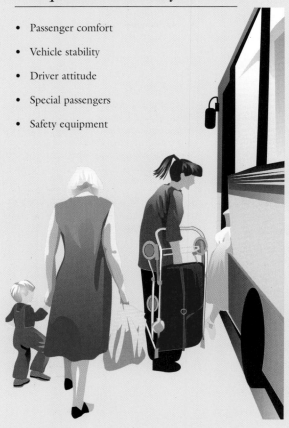

Question

What would you have to be especially aware of when driving a double-decker bus on a road with a steep camber?

Mark one answer

- ☒ **Overhanging trees**
- ☒ Keep Left islands
- ☒ A smooth road surface
- ☒ Pedestrian crossings

Question

For the comfort of your passengers harsh braking should be avoided. You should

Mark one answer

- ☒ **plan ahead and take early action on all stops and hazards**
- ☒ pump the brakes when approaching a bus stop or hazard
- ☒ use the gears to slow down
- ☒ use the handbrake just before stopping to avoid throwing passengers forward

Question

How can you avoid harsh braking?

Mark one answer

- ☒ **Plan ahead and take early action**
- ☒ Gently apply the handbrake
- ☒ Do all the slowing down by using your gears only
- ☒ By pumping the brake pedal several times

Where a road has a steep camber, that is, where the road dips towards the kerb, there are dangers that you must be aware of. As the nearside wheels will be lower this causes the vehicle to lean towards the pavement or verge. You must therefore look out for

- overhanging trees
- lamp-posts
- bus stop roofs

As a driver of a PCV your first priority is the comfort and safety of your passengers. You're delivering a service to paying customers who wish to reach their destination comfortably and safely. Set yourself a high professional standard and take pride in your work.

You must ensure that you have a comprehensive knowledge of *The Highway Code* and other matters relating to vehicle and passenger safety.

Always look well ahead. Early planning and anticipation will help you to avoid braking harshly. As a PCV driver you'll have paying customers on board and they won't want to be thrown forward every time you deal with a hazard.

Question

Which TWO of the following should you do before a bend, roundabout or corner?

Mark two answers

☒ **Select the appropriate gear**

☒ **Adjust your speed**

☒ Indicate

☒ Engage the clutch

☒ Give a hand signal

☒ Check the mirror for passengers

Dealing with hazards late can lead to harsh and erratic steering. This is dangerous for other road users and is also highly uncomfortable for your customers. Assess the situation ahead, adjust your speed accordingly and select the correct gear.

Question

Well ahead of you are traffic lights on green. What should you do in case the lights change to red?

Mark one answer

☒ **Slow down to avoid the need to stop suddenly**

☒ Accelerate to make sure you can cross before they change

☒ Accelerate but warn your passengers you may have to stop

☒ Carry on at a constant speed but be ready to sound your horn

If you're approaching a set of traffic lights and they've been on green for a while, anticipate their changing. Ease off the accelerator and be ready to come to a gradual stop if they change. Don't drive up to them trying to beat the green light. The lights will more than likely change as you come closer, leaving you to brake late and harshly. Think of your passengers.

Question

If a bus takes a bend too fast passengers may be thrown towards

Mark one answer

☒ **the outside of the bend**

☒ the inside of the bend

☒ the front of the bus

☒ the rear of the bus

Turning or travelling around bends under harsh acceleration will push passengers sideways. In addition, the weight of the passengers being transferred to one side of the vehicle will make the vehicle even more unstable. This in turn will make steering out of the bend more difficult.

Question
The driver of a PCV should wear a seat belt if one is fitted UNLESS

Mark two answers

☒ **the vehicle is being reversed**

☒ **a valid medical exemption certificate is held by the driver**

☒ the seat belt is particularly uncomfortable

☒ the belt is of the lap-only type

☒ the passengers carried are children

If your vehicle is fitted with a seat belt you must wear it, unless you're exempt for medical reasons. Seat belts save lives. If the fitting of the belt is uncomfortable and it prevents you obtaining a safe driving position report this to your employer. If it isn't right for you it's likely that it won't be right for other drivers, too.

Question
When seat belts are fitted in a PCV your passengers SHOULD wear them

Mark one answer

☒ **at all times**

☒ on journeys over distances of 25 km (16 miles)

☒ only when travelling in EC countries

☒ only when travelling on motorways

As a driver of a PCV you may be responsible for several passengers at any given time. If a situation occurs where you have to brake or steer harshly in an emergency your passengers could be thrown about the vehicle in different directions. Due to the necessary fittings on board, such as luggage racks, handrails and poles, there's a great danger of injury. If seat belts are provided for passengers they should wear them. Seat belts save lives.

Question
Which of the following is a legal requirement for every PCV?

Mark one answer

☒ **A fire extinguisher**

☒ A current timetable

☒ A mobile phone or radio

☒ A working tachograph

Every PCV must carry a fire extinguisher. Make sure that you know where it's located and how to use it so that you're fully prepared in the event of a fire.

Question
If a passenger carries a white stick with red rings painted on it this shows the person is

Mark one answer

☒ blind and deaf

☒ deaf only

☒ unable to climb steps

☒ blind only

Question
A passenger finds walking difficult.
What could you do to help?

Mark one answer

☒ Wait until the passenger is sitting down before moving away

☒ Reduce the time spent on the bus by driving more quickly

☒ Make sure they have a window seat

☒ Suggest they stand near the door

Give extra care to those passengers who require more time or help to get on or off the vehicle. Recognise their disability and help them as much as you can.

There's a great deal of competition these days and passengers often have a choice of how they travel. Take pride in your work and this will show through in the way that you deal with your passengers. They'll appreciate this and travel with your company again.

You should always try to wait until your passengers have become seated before you move away. This is even more important if a passenger is elderly or has difficulty walking.

There are several ways that you, the driver, can make a journey easier for people with disabilities. There are several devices that can be fitted to vehicles to make getting on and off easier. Wide doors and lifting devices will help wheelchair access. But don't forget the personal touch. Offer help when you think it might be needed. And remember, a smile goes a long way.

DSA THEORY TEST for large vehicle drivers

Question

This sign fitted to the front and rear of a PCV means that

Mark one answer

✗ **the PCV may be carrying children**

☒ children must be accompanied by an adult

☒ the bus is carrying blind people

☒ the driver will help disabled people

If you're carrying children on your vehicle and it isn't on a scheduled route used by the general public it must have a sign displayed to the front and rear.

When carrying children to and from school it's likely that you'll have to make several stops in places other than recognised bus stops. Think carefully before you stop. Don't cause unnecessary inconvenience to other road users.

Question

Hazard warning lights may only be used at certain times.
In addition, a PCV displaying this sign may use them when

Mark one answer

✗ **stopped and children are getting on or off the vehicle**

☒ stopped at a pedestrian crossing

☒ approaching a school crossing patrol

☒ there's a sign warning of a school ahead

You may be driving in the rush hour, when traffic is dense, so when you stop you're permitted to show your hazard warning lights. This will show other road users that children are getting on and off the vehicle. Look out for passing traffic and try to ensure that all your passengers get on and off safely.

This section looks at how to behave in the event of an accident.

The questions will ask you about

- Reducing risk

- Injuries

- Hazardous materials

- Casualties

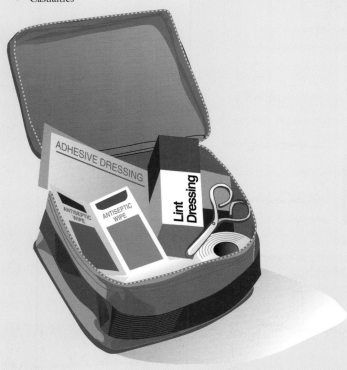

Question
In the UK the headroom under bridges, unless otherwise shown, is AT LEAST

Mark one answer

☒ **5 metres (16 feet 6 inches)**

☒ 4.8 metres (16 feet)

☒ 6 metres (19 feet 8 inches)

☒ 8 metres (26 feet 3 inches)

Question
You're approaching a bridge that has NO height restriction on it.
The height of the bridge will be at least

Mark one answer

☒ **5 metres (16 feet 6 inches)**

☒ 4.4 metres (14 feet 5 inches)

☒ 4.8 metres (16 feet)

☒ 3.6 metres (11 feet 10 inches)

Question
Your PCV hits a low railway bridge. Nobody is injured.
You should report the accident

Mark one answer

☒ **immediately, to Railtrack**

☒ immediately, to your employer

☒ within 24 hours to Railtrack

☒ within seven days to the police

Always be aware of the height of the vehicle you're driving. Don't forget you're driving a high vehicle – there are over 750 incidents a year involving collisions with railway bridges. Every effort should be made to prevent these incidents occuring. If you do hit a railway bridge it must be reported to

- Railtrack or Northern Ireland Railways (NIR)
- the police

You must report the accident facts to the police as soon as possible, or at least within 24 hours. Failure to report an incident involving a railway bridge is an offence.

Due to the possibility of structural damage to the bridge it's highly recommended that you inform the authorities immediately. You should telephone Railtrack's 24-hour bridge hotline number 0345 003 355 and report the incident. It's very important to do this as soon as possible so that all rail traffic is stopped.

In Northern Ireland you **must** report it to NIR and the police immediately.

Question
What must you do if you're involved in an accident?

Mark one answer
✖ Stop at the scene of the accident

☒ Drive on for help

☒ Inform the police within seven days

☒ Drive to the nearest police station

Question
Your vehicle has been involved in an accident where someone is injured. You don't produce the required insurance certificate at the time of the accident.
You must report the accident to the police as soon as possible, or in any case within

Mark one answer
✖ 24 hours

☒ 48 hours

☒ 72 hours

☒ seven days

Question
Your PCV has hit a parked vehicle. The owner can't be found.
You must report the accident

Mark one answer
✖ to the police within 24 hours

☒ to the police within seven days

☒ to the owner as soon as possible

☒ to the owner within seven days

If your vehicle is involved in an accident you must stop. If the accident causes any damage or injury to another person, other vehicle, any animal not in your vehicle, or roadside property you must

- stop at the scene
- give your own address and the vehicle owner's address, plus the registration number of the vehicle to anyone having reasonable grounds to require it

If you don't give your name and address at the time of the accident, report the accident to the police as soon as reasonably practicable. That is, as soon as possible, or in any case within 24 hours.

If any other person is injured and you don't produce your insurance at the time of the accident to the police or to any other person who has reasonable grounds to request it, you must also

- report the accident to the police as soon as possible, or in any case within 24 hours
- produce your insurance certificate to the police either when reporting the accident or within seven days (five days in Northern Ireland) at any police station you select

If you damage a parked vehicle and the owner isn't around you must report this to the police. This applies to any property you might have damaged.

In Northern Ireland all accidents must be reported to the police forthwith.

DSA THEORY TEST for large vehicle drivers

Question

At the scene of an accident you see a plain orange rectangle displayed on one of the vehicles.

This tells you that the vehicle

Mark one answer

☒ **is carrying hazardous material**

☐ is carrying a First Aid kit

☐ is carrying medical supplies

☐ is unladen

Question

You're treating a passenger who's in shock. You should

Mark one answer

☒ **keep them warm**

☐ give them liquids

☐ keep them moving

☐ encourage them to sleep

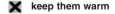

Question

Your PCV is involved in an accident. You have a passenger who's unconscious but still breathing.

What should you do?

Mark one answer

☒ **Get medical help**

☐ Check their pulse

☐ Give them liquid

☐ Lie them on their back

Vehicles that carry hazardous goods have badges displayed on the side and rear. These are coloured orange and show the type of material that's being carried. Make a note of this and report it to the emergency services when you contact them.

Knowing what to do in the event of an accident could save lives. Stay calm and be in command of the situation. Call the emergency services. They're the experts and know how to deal with injured or shocked victims. First Aid is very important, but the correct procedure is vital.

Although not obviously injured, passengers may be suffering from shock. Reassure them and keep them warm. Don't give them anything to eat or drink.

If one of your passengers is unconscious but breathing, get medical help immediately. Only move the casualty if there's danger of further injury. Call the experts: dial 999.

Study the section on First Aid in your copy of *The Goods Vehicle Driving Manual* or *The Bus and Coach Driving Manual*. Please note that the advice given in these manuals is only a brief example of how you may deal with situations on the road. If you require further and more comprehensive details about First Aid you can contact the

- St John Ambulance Association and Brigade
- St Andrew's Ambulance Association
- British Red Cross Association

There's no substitute for proper training.

SECTION 6 VEHICLE CONDITION

This section looks at the condition of your vehicle.

The questions will ask you about

- Safety checks
- Legal requirements

Question
Which THREE of the following items would
make a tyre illegal for a large goods vehicle?

Mark three answers

☒ **A lump or bulge**

☒ **A deep cut more than 25 mm (1 inch)
long**

☒ **An exposed ply or cord**

☒ Recut tyres

☒ A tread depth of 1.3 mm

☒ Different makes of tyres on the same
axle

Question
You notice that two wheel nuts are missing
from one of the wheels.
What should you do?

Mark one answer

☒ **Park and phone for assistance**

☒ Continue your journey

☒ Drive to the nearest tyre depot

☒ Use a nut from another wheel

You should carry out checks on your tyres as
part of your routine check of the vehicle.

A damaged or worn tyre can have major
effects on the handling of your vehicle.
In no circumstances should your tyres ever
show any cord. The cord is found just below
a tyre's rubber surface. A severely worn tyre
like this is a greater safety risk. Check that
the tread depth is at least 1 mm and that
there aren't any bulges or cuts in the side
walls. Check ALL the tyres, and the inside
walls, too.

If there's a lump or bulge in the tyre it must
be changed immediately. Your vehicle will
be a danger on the road if you drive it with
defective tyres. It's also an offence to drive
with defective tyres.

If you notice any missing wheel nuts, park
and phone for assistance. It's essential that
wheel fixings are tightened to the torque
specified by the manufacturer, with the
approved calibrated torque wrench.

As a professional driver you must ensure that
your vehicle is in serviceable condition at all
times. Checks should be made before you
leave on any journey, but make a visual
check every time you start up again after a
rest stop. Don't take risks by driving a
defective vehicle, however important your
journey may seem at the time.

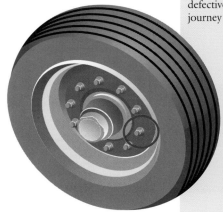

Question

In very cold weather moisture may freeze in your vehicle's air storage tanks.
Which of the following would help to prevent this?

Mark one answer

☒ **Draining the tanks daily**

☒ Covering the air tanks with a blanket

☒ Using the brakes frequently

☒ Pumping the brakes

In very cold weather moisture can build up in the storage tanks and freeze. Ice can form in the pipes and this will result in loss of pressure or, worse, brake failure. Make sure that you drain the tanks daily as part of a routine. Most modern vehicles are fitted with automatic bleed valves. Check that they're working properly and that air drying systems are effective.

Question

Side reflectors must be fitted to trailers if they're longer than

Mark one answer

☒ **5 metres (16 feet 6 inches)**

☒ 6 metres (19 feet 8 inches)

☒ 8 metres (26 feet 3 inches)

☒ 10 metres (33 feet)

New trailers must be fitted with side reflectors if they're over 5 metres (16 feet 6 inches). Make sure that they aren't broken and that they're kept clean.

Question

What does this warning light on the instrument panel mean?

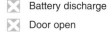

Mark one answer

☒ **Braking system fault**

☒ Low oil pressure

☒ Battery discharge

☒ Door open

You should be familiar with all warning lights and buzzers fitted to your vehicle. If you're driving the vehicle for the first time ensure that you know the function of each. If the brake warning light indicates a fault in the system stop as soon as it's safe to do so. Report the fault and don't continue until the fault has been corrected.

Question

You're driving an LGV along a motorway. You notice that tread is coming away from one of your tyres.
What should you do?

Mark one answer

✖ **Stop on the hard shoulder and phone for assistance**

▨ Stop on the hard shoulder and change the wheel

▨ Continue driving to the next service station

▨ Continue driving and leave by the next exit

It's dangerous to drive a defective vehicle. Continuous high speeds on the motorway can cause the tyres to become hot and shred. If you notice this in your mirrors you must stop on the hard shoulder as soon as it's safe to do so.

If you're on a motorway and you notice any defect on your vehicle you must stop on the hard shoulder as soon as it's safe. Use the emergency telephone for assistance.

Question
You're driving an LGV. Your power-assisted steering has suddenly failed.
What should you do?

Mark one answer

☒ **Park and seek assistance**

☒ Continue driving to the nearest repair centre

☒ Return to the depot

☒ Continue your journey at a slower speed

Question
You're driving a rigid LGV. Your steering suddenly becomes heavy to turn.
What could this indicate?

Mark two answers

☒ **A failure of power-assisted steering**

☒ **A puncture in a front tyre**

☒ Loss of air pressure

☒ A faulty handbrake

Question
What should you do if the brake pedal becomes 'hard'?

Mark one answer

☒ **Park and telephone for assistance**

☒ Continue to drive and report it at the end of the day

☒ Pump the brake pedal continuously

☒ Drain the air tanks and then continue

Power steering is designed to help the driver by reducing the effort required to turn the steering wheel. It uses hydraulic pressure to assist with the steering mechanism. Hydraulic fluid is pressured by a pump that's driven by the vehicle's engine. The power-assisted steering only operates when the engine is running. If this system fails the steering will become very stiff and difficult to turn. It may also be felt as a series of jerks.

You should park and seek assistance. The vehicle is designed to be used with this steering assistance and driving the vehicle without it might cause danger to other road users.

If the steering becomes heavy there are other possible causes you should be aware of. Your vehicle might have a puncture or the load might have shifted. In any case you should stop safely, investigate the cause, then seek assistance.

Don't take risks. As soon as you detect a fault on your vehicle you must take action. Where the brakes are concerned always park and get assistance. Always report minor faults as soon as you detect them. Minor faults can become major ones if they aren't seen to quickly.

Question
Your vehicle is fitted with a warning device, which sounds when reversing.
When should you NOT use it in a built-up area?

Mark one answer

☒ **Between 11.30 pm and 7 am**

☒ Between 12.30 am and 8 am

☒ Between 10.30 pm and 6.30 am

☒ Between 11 pm and 6.30 am

Some modern vehicles are fitted with an audible warning that sounds when the vehicle's reversing. This is an effective device to warn pedestrians and others of a reversing vehicle. This doesn't take away the need, however, to use effective observation around your vehicle before and while you're reversing.

Don't use this device in built-up areas at night. Have some consideration for the residents and don't disturb them with excessive noise.

Question
On a double-deck PCV what depth of tyre tread is required over three-quarters of its width?

Mark one answer

☒ **1 mm**

☒ 0.8 mm

☒ 1.6 mm

☒ 2 mm

It's essential that the tyres on your vehicle are in good condition. You must never forget that you have passengers on board. Their safety must be your priority. At no time should the depth of the tread be less than 1 mm over three-quarters of the width of the tyre.

Question
What's the MINIMUM depth of tread required over three-quarters of the breadth of an LGV tyre?

Mark one answer

☒ **1 mm**

☒ 1.5 mm

☒ 2.5 mm

☒ 5 mm

Your tyres are the only contact with the road. It's essential that this contact gives you the grip you need to control your vehicle at all times. If the weather is wet or icy you'll be relying on your tyres to a greater degree.

Question
How much of the width of a tyre must have the legal limit of tread depth?

Mark one answer

☒ **Three-quarters**

☒ One half

☒ One-quarter

☒ Five-eighths

The condition of the tyres on your vehicle will contribute to its overall stability. Don't leave your tyres until they're at the minimum depth. Renew them before they get into that state. Ensure that the tread is always deep enough, thus reducing the risk to road safety.

Question
How frequently must a walk-around check be done?

Mark one answer

☒ **Daily**

☒ Weekly

☒ Every 100 miles

☒ Every 1,000 miles

Check your vehicle daily as a routine. Your vehicle should be in a good condition at all times. A badly maintained vehicle could be illegal, as well as a danger to your passengers and other road users. Get into the habit of making a visual check before you move off after rest stops, as well as before your journey.

Question

How long must a driver's defect report be kept?

Mark one answer

☒ **15 months**

☒ Six months

☒ 12 months

☒ 18 months

Always report a fault at the earliest opportunity. Small faults can become large or dangerous ones if they aren't reported early enough. Regular maintenance will ensure that your vehicle is safe and will prolong its life.

Records of safety inspections must be kept for at least 15 months, and they should be available for inspection.

In Northern Ireland there's no legal requirement for safety inspection records to be kept.

This section looks at safety when leaving your vehicle.

The questions will ask you about

- Mirrors and signals

- Passenger comfort

- Driver's cab

Question
As driver of a PCV your FIRST priority is

Mark one answer

❌ **the safety and comfort of your passengers**

☒ making sure that you're always on time

☒ making sure that your log book and tachograph are correctly completed

☒ making sure that your destination is clearly marked

As a driver of a passenger carrying vehicle you have responsibilities beyond those of other drivers. Your passengers have paid for a service and should arrive at their chosen destination safely. By providing a courteous and comfortable service your customers will travel with you again.

Question
The driver of a one-person-operated double-decker bus should be constantly aware of passengers on the top deck.
How should this be done?

Mark one answer

❌ **By making full use of the internal mirror system**

☒ By counting passengers up and down the staircase

☒ By frequent checks upstairs while stopped at bus stops

☒ By listening to passengers in the upstairs gangway when approaching bus stops

If you're driving a one-person-operated double-decker bus you must ensure that you're able to see passengers who are about to descend the stairs. Make sure that you can see them in the internal mirrors. Always consider their safety, and avoid harsh braking and steering.

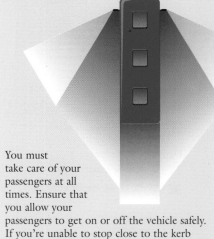

Question
A bus stop is blocked and you can't pull into it. Before opening the exit door what's the most important action to take?

Mark one answer

❌ **Check for traffic on the left**

☒ Try to get the bus stop cleared

☒ Carry on to the next bus stop

☒ Check for traffic on the right

You must take care of your passengers at all times. Ensure that you allow your passengers to get on or off the vehicle safely. If you're unable to stop close to the kerb don't open the doors until you're sure it's safe. Always check the nearside mirror before you do this.

Question
Passengers may be in a hurry to get off the bus as you approach a bus stop.
What should you do to reduce any dangers?

Mark one answer

☒ Not open the passenger doors until the bus stops

☒ Insist that passengers stay seated until the bus stops

☒ Pull up just before the stop and let passengers get off

☒ Let passengers on the bus before letting passengers off

Question
This PCV has a separate door for the driver, opening onto the offside.
What should the driver do when getting out of such a vehicle?
Choose TWO of the following.

Mark two answers

☒ Check for passing traffic

☒ Climb down backwards using the footholds

☒ Climb down forwards using the footholds

☒ Jump down carefully, flexing the knees on landing

☒ Climb down holding the steering wheel rim tightly

Passengers may be in a hurry to get off at their stop. Don't

• brake harshly
• open the doors until the vehicle has come to a stop

as passengers may have left their seats early and might be standing up, waiting to get off. Due to the necessary fittings on board, such as handrails, poles and luggage racks, there's a greater risk of injury. Consider your passengers' safety first.

If your vehicle has a separate offside driver's door you must take the precaution of good observation before leaving the vehicle. Don't jump down out of the cab. Leave by climbing down facing towards the vehicle. Consider your own safety as well as that of others. Always check for close passing traffic before getting out of your vehicle.

DSA THEORY TEST for large vehicle drivers

Question

You've just parked an LGV at a roadside in very heavy traffic.
Before dismounting from the cab you should be particularly careful to do which one of the following?

Mark one answer

☒ Check the rear view mirrors

☒ Make sure the radio is turned down

☒ Make sure the hazard warning lights are on

☒ Check that all windows are closed

Dismounting from the offside of a vehicle can be hazardous, especially if the traffic is travelling at speed. Lean out of the window and use your mirrors to check behind and all around the vehicle. Ensure that you use all proper footholds and hand grips. Be responsible for your own health and safety.

Question

Drivers of tanker vehicles must exercise special care when climbing on to walkways to gain access to tank hatches.
The dangers they need to be aware of include

Mark three answers

☒ slipping off

☒ overhead cables

☒ overhead pipeways

☒ distracting other drivers

☒ walkways not being wide enough

☒ ladders not being properly secured

Take your time if you're using walkways at high levels. Fuel can make the surface slippery and therefore increase the safety risk.

Hazard warning lights may be used in which TWO of these situations?

Mark two answers

☒ **When driving on motorways or dual carriageways to warn following drivers of a hazard ahead**

☒ **When your vehicle is stopped to warn others of an obstruction**

☒ To thank a driver who has let you pull in

☒ As a warning to drivers that you're towing another vehicle

☒ To show your intention to go ahead at a junction when your position might suggest otherwise

Use the hazard warning lights if you're approaching a queue of traffic on the motorway. This will alert traffic behind, which might not be able to see the hazard due to the bulk of your vehicle.

Don't use your hazard warning lights as an excuse for illegal parking. They should only be used for warning other road users of a hazard ahead, not one created by your thoughtless parking.

This section looks at vehicle loading.

The questions will ask you about

- Passenger safety
- Legal requirements

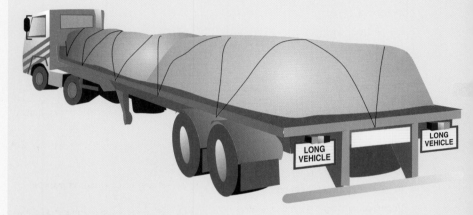

Question

When driving, on which TWO occasions would you be most likely to experience weight transfer?

Mark two answers

☒ **Braking**

☒ **Cornering**

☒ Reversing

☒ Overtaking

☒ Unloading

☒ Loading

Question

Why is it important to distribute the weight evenly over the axles when loading an LGV?

Mark one answer

☒ **To ensure maximum stability**

☒ To ensure easy unloading

☒ To make it easier to sheet up

☒ To ensure maximum ground clearance

Question

Which of the following is most important when loading a vehicle?

Mark one answer

☒ **Spreading the load evenly**

☒ Loading it towards the rear

☒ Loading it towards the front

☒ Loading it towards the centre

You must take extra care when your vehicle is carrying a load. When braking or cornering the vehicle's weight will transfer. When

• cornering, weight will be transferred away from the direction in which you're turning

• braking, weight can be transferred in several different directions

A vehicle should be loaded so that the weight of a load is evenly distributed over the axles. This will increase the stability of the load.

In addition, when driving you should brake

• in good time

• in a straight line wherever possible

Look well ahead so that you can avoid harsh braking. Always reduce your speed before you make a turn so that you aren't braking and steering at the same time.

Question
An LGV is found to be overloaded.
Who's liable to be prosecuted for this offence?

Mark one answer

✗ Both the driver and the operator

☒ The people who loaded the vehicle

☒ The operator only

☒ The driver only

Before you leave on a journey always check that your load is secure. Do this after a rest stop, too. You and your operator are both responsible if your vehicle is overloaded.

Question
Why is it a legal requirement to sheet a loose load on an LGV?

Mark one answer

✗ To stop the load from blowing away

☒ To stop handling being affected

☒ To stop the load from shifting

☒ To aid other drivers' vision

If you're carrying a load that consists of loose materials it must be securely roped and sheeted. You must not risk the chance of losing any part of your load. This could cause damage to other road users and you'll be held responsible.

After stops, keep a check in your mirrors as you're driving to ensure that the sheet is secure. Air can force itself under the sheet and work it loose.

Question
When roping down a load on your LGV what's the best knot to use?

Mark one answer

✗ A dolly knot

☒ A reef knot

☒ A slip knot

☒ A bowline knot

If a load is being secured by ropes you must ensure that they're tied securely to the body of the unit. The most effective method of tying is by 'dolly knots'. These are non-slip knots that hold firmly. You should practise tying these and use them appropriately.

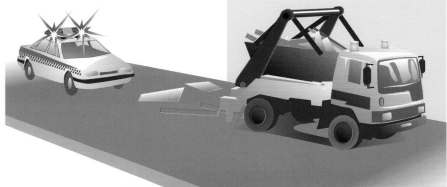

DSA THEORY TEST for large vehicle drivers

Question
You must fit marker boards if your load overhangs the rear of your vehicle by more than

Mark one answer

✖ **2 metres (6 feet 6 inches)**

☒ 1.5 metres (5 feet)

☒ 2.5 metres (8 feet 2 inches)

☒ 3 metres (9 feet 10 inches)

You must always fit marker boards to your vehicle if the load overhangs by more than 2 metres (6 feet 6 inches). These must be clean and lit in bad visibility or at night.

Question
The load on an LGV becomes insecure on a journey.
The driver should

Mark one answer

✖ **park and resecure the load before continuing**

☒ continue at a slower speed to ensure the load doesn't fall off

☒ attach 'hazard' boards to warn other road users

☒ inform base at the earliest opportunity

If you become aware that any part of your load is insecure you must stop as soon as it's safe to do so. Re-secure the load before continuing on your journey. If this isn't possible then you must seek assistance. Don't take risks.

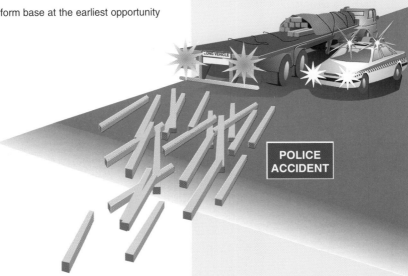

Question

When on a journey you should check your load

Mark one answer

 **at regular intervals**

when travelling in windy conditions

when travelling at night

when travelling in wet conditions

Every time you stop for a break take the time to walk around your vehicle and check that all the ropes or devices are secure. If the load is sheeted check that it isn't loose. Air can become trapped under loose sheeting, causing it to lift away from the load. Check the load at regular intervals, as sheeting can loosen from time to time.

Question

How many people can you have standing on the upper deck of a double-decker bus?

Mark one answer

 None

Two

Five

Ten

Double-decker buses are provided with internal mirrors so that the driver can see the passengers at the top of the stairs. You should be aware that passengers may get up from their seats and descend the stairs some distance from their stop. Standing passengers are less stable and for this reason they aren't allowed to travel on the top deck without a seat.

Question

You're approaching a bus stop with people standing ready to get off your bus. You should

Mark one answer

 brake gently

clutch coast

change gear

brake hard

Always brake gently as you approach a bus stop. Those passengers waiting to get off will be standing and could lose their balance.

Question

What's the likely weight difference between an empty bus and a bus with 75 passengers on board?

Mark one answer

✗ **5 tonnes**

☒ 6 tonnes

☒ 10 tonnes

☒ 19 tonnes

The way that your vehicle handles will differ greatly when it's full as opposed to when it's empty. A bus with 75 passengers on board could increase the weight by up to about 5 tonnes. The passengers may also be carrying luggage, either with them or in a luggage compartment. The extra weight will have an effect on inertia and momentum. It will take longer to build up speed but the vehicle will maintain forward momentum, requiring controlled braking.

This section looks at the subject of restricted views when driving a large vehicle.

The questions will ask you about

- Mirrors

- Signals

- Parking

- Moving off

- Blind spots

- Observation at junctions

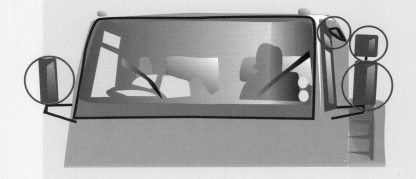

Question
What should you first check before moving to the LEFT?

Mark one answer

✗ The nearside mirror

☒ The offside mirror

☒ Behind, over your right shoulder

☒ Behind, over your left shoulder

Question
What should you first check before moving to the RIGHT?

Mark one answer

✗ The offside mirror

☒ The nearside mirror

☒ Behind, over your left shoulder

☒ Behind, over your right shoulder

Question
You're about to move off.
You should always

Mark one answer

✗ use your mirrors and look behind

☒ extend your right arm as far as you can out of the window

☒ use only the offside mirror and move away quickly

☒ signal right with indicator and arm together

The left side of the vehicle, as you face forwards, is often referred to as the nearside; the right side of the vehicle as the offside. Before you make a turn or a change of direction, however slight, you should always check the mirrors. If you intend to turn left, check your left-hand (nearside) mirror first, then your right-hand (offside) mirror, and then your left mirror again as you turn. If you intend to turn right, check your right-hand (offside) mirror first, then your left-hand (nearside) mirror, and then your right mirror again as you turn.

You must ensure that all your mirrors are properly adjusted to give a clear view around and behind. They should be free from dirt and grime and at no time be broken.

You must use the mirrors well before you signal your intention to make any manoeuvre. Use them before

- moving away
- changing direction
- turning left or right
- overtaking
- changing lanes
- slowing or stopping
- speeding up
- opening the cab door

Looking into your mirrors isn't enough. You must act correctly and positively on what you see. Develop a routine that will give you a constant update on what's happening around your vehicle.
Using your mirrors is essential but you must also look behind. There might be a vehicle, pedestrian or cyclist that you haven't seen in your mirrors.

Question
In which THREE of the following situations would you FIRST need to check your nearside mirror?

Mark three answers

❌ **After passing cars on your left**

❌ **Before moving to the left**

❌ **After passing pedestrians standing on the nearside kerb**

☒ Before moving out to pass a car parked on your left

☒ Before moving out to the right

On a large vehicle the nearside mirror is very important and it's essential to use it when moving off. You must check for pedestrians and cyclists along the nearside of your vehicle. Passengers might be running for a bus or waiting very close to the kerbside. Cyclists might ride up along your nearside while you're stationary.

As you pass vehicles on the left you should ensure that you check your mirror and leave a safety margin before you move back to the left. This applies whether the vehicles are stationary or moving.

Question
The MSM routine is used to negotiate a hazard. What do the initials MSM stand for?

Mark one answer

❌ **Mirror, signal, manoeuvre**

☒ Manoeuvre, speed, mirror

☒ Mirror, speed, manoeuvre

☒ Manoeuvre, signal, mirror

A 'hazard' is any situation that could involve adjusting speed or altering course. Look well ahead so that you're ready to deal with them in good time. Always use the MSM routine when you're approaching a hazard.

M – Mirrors
Check the position of the traffic behind you.

S – Signal
Signal your intention to slow down or change course in good time.

M – Manoeuvre
A manoeuvre is any change in position, from slowing or stopping the vehicle to turning off a busy road.

Question
You want to park a semi-trailer and leave it unattended.
Where should you NOT do this?

Mark one answer

❌ **In a lay-by**

☒ In a lorry park

☒ On level ground

☒ In a factory

If you need to park the semi-trailer of your vehicle find a safe place. Don't park it in a lay-by. Leave these available for drivers who wish to stop and rest. Find a place off the road, preferably a lorry park or somewhere safe which will decrease the risk of theft.

Check that the ground is firm and level before you uncouple the trailer. If you need to, place a heavy plank under the legs to distribute the weight and stop the legs sinking into the ground.

Question
When parking an LGV at night where must you have lights on?

Mark one answer

✖ **On the road**

☒ In a motorway service area

☒ In a factory entrance

☒ In dock authority areas

If you have to stop for a short while in a lay-by you should always leave the side lights on. The lay-by might be away from street lighting and other vehicles entering the lay-by must be able to see your vehicle. You must always leave your side lights on when parked on the road.

Question
You're driving an LGV. You're about to move off from behind a stationary car.
What should you do?
Choose THREE of the following.

Mark three answers

✖ **Signal before moving**

✖ **Check the blind spot before moving**

✖ **Use both mirrors before moving**

☒ Start to signal when moving

☒ Use both mirrors only after moving

Because the body of your vehicle is designed to take loads your view around it will be restricted. Take extra care to look well out of the window to check the blind spots. Don't forget to check all the mirrors. Check ahead and signal if necessary before moving off.

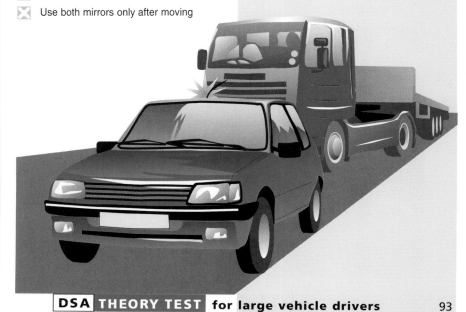

Question
What does this sign mean?

Mark one answer

☒ **With-flow bus and cycle lane**

☒ Contraflow bus and cycle lane

☒ No buses or cycles

☒ Priority to buses or cycles

In some towns there are special lanes set aside for certain types of vehicle. These lanes show a picture of, or state, the authorised road users and there's usually a sign showing the time that the lane is in operation. Some lanes might only be in operation for a short time. Check the sign and use the lane only if it's permitted.

Question
You're driving in fast-moving traffic along a motorway. There's a stationary queue of traffic ahead. What should you do?

Mark one answer

☒ **Switch on your hazard warning lights**

☒ Move to the hard shoulder

☒ Change lanes

☒ Give a slowing down signal

Traffic queues on the motorway are becoming more common, whether due to the sheer volume of traffic at peak times or an incident. Keep well back from the vehicle in front so you'll be able to see the problems ahead on the road. If you see a queue of stationary traffic ahead, switching on your hazard warning lights will warn those behind you of the approaching hazard.

Question

You're driving a PCV 12 metres (39 feet 4 inches) long. You want to turn right at a roundabout. There are TWO LANES marked for turning right. You should

Mark one answer

✘ **use the left-hand of the two lanes**

☒ use the right-hand of the two lanes

☒ use either lane

☒ straddle the two lanes

If there are two lanes for a right turn at a roundabout and you're driving a long vehicle, take the left-hand of the two lanes as you approach. This will allow you room to negotiate the roundabout without mounting or scuffing the kerb. Keep a check in the right-hand mirror as the rear end of the vehicle might cut across the right-hand lane when you steer around the roundabout.

Question

You're driving a long articulated vehicle. Your view is restricted by buildings and parked cars. How should you turn right out of a T-junction?

Mark one answer

✘ **Ease forward slowly until you have a clear view**

☒ Look both ways at the same time as emerging

☒ Sound your horn while emerging to warn other vehicles

☒ Emerge quickly to clear the junction

If your view at a junction is restricted by parked vehicles you should ease forward slowly until you can see.

IF YOU DON'T KNOW, DON'T GO.

Your vehicle takes longer than a car to gather speed so you won't be able to accelerate out of trouble. Don't impede the progress of the traffic in the road that you're turning into.

Question

You're crossing a dual carriageway to turn right. Your vehicle is too long for the gap. How should you proceed?

Mark one answer

✘ **Wait until it's clear from both directions**

☒ Move forward and wait in the middle

☒ Turn left and find another route

☒ Look both ways at the same time as emerging

If you wish to turn right onto a dual carriageway don't stop in the middle unless the gap is big enough for your vehicle to do so without impeding the moving traffic. Consider turning left and using a roundabout further on up the road to avoid crossing the central reservation.

Question

You want to turn left at a road junction. What's most important when deciding your position?
Choose THREE of the following.

Mark three answers

✗ The length of the vehicle

✗ The width of the roads

✗ The angle of the corner

☒ The camber of the road

☒ The type of road surface

Question

As you're driving your vehicle a group of horse riders comes towards you. The leading rider's horse has suddenly become nervous of your presence.
What should you do?

Mark one answer

✗ Brake gently to a stop until they've passed

☒ Brake quickly to a stop, applying the handbrake

☒ Continue driving, keeping well in to the nearside

☒ Increase speed to pass the riders quickly

Where you position your vehicle on approach to a left turn will depend on several factors. You should be considering and deciding on the best position as you approach. If you need to take up part of any other lane be extra cautious. Other road users might not understand your reasons for doing this. They might try to pass on the left in the gap that you need to make the turn. Always check the left-hand mirror as you approach and just before you turn. It's better to take extra road space on the road that you're leaving than to expect there to be extra room on the road that you're entering. There might not be any.

If you have to pass a group of riders on horseback you must give them plenty of room. Try not to startle the animals – the riders might be learners and have limited control. If any of the animals do become unsettled you should brake gently and come to a stop. A nervous animal is unpredictable; you should wait until the animal is settled or has passed by.

Other road users behind you might have limited vision of the hazard, so good mirror work and early signalling will be required.

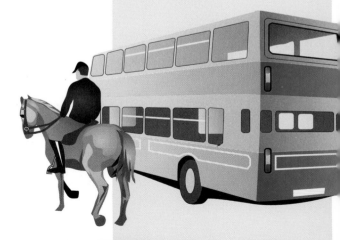

DSA **THEORY TEST** for large vehicle drivers

Question

To have good all-round vision you should make sure that

Mark one answer

☒ **your seat is properly adjusted**

☒ windows are open

☒ a sun visor is fitted

☒ all lights are clean

Question

In a PCV with a high driving position you may have to look out for

Mark one answer

☒ **cyclists close in front**

☒ cyclists close behind

☒ large vehicles close in front

☒ large vehicles close behind

Large vehicles are designed for their specific function and this often means the shape and size can impair all-round visibility for the driver. You must make sure that you adjust the seat so that you're able to reach all the controls and see in all the mirrors. You should be seated in such a way so that you're able to lean out of the window and check all offside blind spots.

It's essential that you're constantly aware of other road users and pedestrians around you. A routine of effective mirror checking should be achieved. You must also know when it's essential to make checks in the blind spots, such as just below the nearside front of the vehicle. A cyclist in that space could be out of your normal vision area. Constant awareness will ensure that you've seen any riders getting into that position.

Question

Some large vehicles with restricted vision to the rear may be fitted with an audible warning device for reversing.

In areas with a 30 mph (48 kph) restriction the device may be used

Mark one answer

✗ **between 7 am and 11.30 pm only**

☒ between 11.30 pm and 7 am only

☒ during hours of daylight only

☒ at any time

Some vehicles are fitted with an audible warning device that sounds when the vehicle is being reversed. This is an effective safety feature but doesn't take away the need to use good, effective observation around the vehicle before and while reversing. As these devices make a loud sound they shouldn't be used between 11.30 pm and 7 am.

CAUTION! Vehicle reversing

Question

What would you do if smoke started coming from the exhaust system, making it difficult for others to see?

Mark one answer

✗ **Stop and get the fault fixed immediately**

☒ Carry on driving

☒ Drive back to your depot

☒ Let the engine cool down

You should respect the environment and try to keep excessive noise and exhaust fumes to a minimum. Smoke from the exhaust is unpleasant and could indicate a fault with the vehicle, which should be checked as soon as possible. If smoke from the exhaust system does become a problem, do the responsible and professional thing – stop and seek assistance to get the fault mended straight away.

DSA **THEORY TEST** for large vehicle drivers

Question
Driving too close to the vehicle in front will

Mark one answer

☒ **decrease your view ahead**

☒ increase your view ahead

☒ increase the view of following drivers

☒ decrease the view of following drivers

Question
The 'turning circle' is the

Mark one answer

☒ **amount of space needed for the vehicle to turn**

☒ number of turns of the steering wheel between locks

☒ amount by which the vehicle overhangs kerbs

☒ amount by which a vehicle cuts corners

At all times, you must be aware that as a driver of a large vehicle you won't be able to see all around the vehicle. This is why you must have an excellent mirror routine and be constantly updating your information on what's going on around you. Don't get into a position where you reduce your vision unnecessarily, such as driving too close to the vehicle in front.

You should be familiar with the room that your vehicle requires to make turns or carry out a manoeuvre. You'll need to consider this as you approach junctions and road layouts. If you're driving a new or temporary vehicle, familiarise yourself with its characteristics before you drive on public roads.

This section looks at precautions to take when overtaking.

The questions will ask you about

- Lane discipline

- Observation

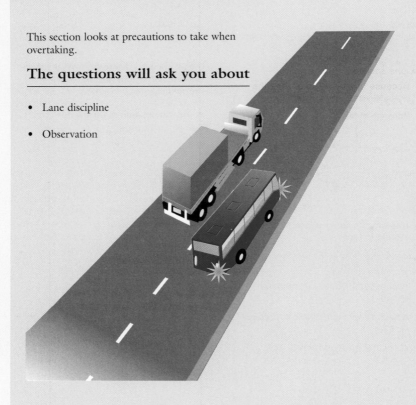

Question
As an LGV driver, why must you always have a long, clear road ahead before you consider overtaking another vehicle?

Mark one answer

❌ **Because of the length of time the manoeuvre will take**

☒ Because of the effect of the vehicle's speed limit

☒ Because of the stopping distances involved

☒ Because of the possibility of 'dead ground'

Question
On a motorway what do signs showing a crawler lane for LGVs suggest?

Mark one answer

❌ **There will be a long, gradual hill ahead**

☒ Advance warning for a steep downhill section

☒ LGVs and PCVs are limited to use of that lane

☒ Vehicles other than LGVs and PCVs are banned from that lane

Question
What is a crawler lane designed for?

Mark one answer

❌ **To enable slow-moving traffic to move further over to the left on uphill gradients**

☒ To enable other traffic to overtake on the nearside

☒ To enable LGVs to pull over and park out of the way

☒ To enable emergency vehicles to get to the scene of an accident quicker

Before you overtake another vehicle there are several things to consider. Due to the size and weight of your vehicle you'll need a long, clear road ahead before you attempt the manoeuvre. There are several factors to think about, but first ask yourself if overtaking is really necessary. Consider

• the power limitations of your vehicle
• oncoming traffic
• bends
• junctions
• road markings
• traffic signs
• gradients
• other traffic

You'll have to use your skill and judgement to assess the situation and decide whether you can overtake safely. If you see a crawler lane sign ahead this would indicate an uphill gradient. You shouldn't attempt any manoeuvre that would require an increase in speed, such as overtaking. The combination of a heavy load, a speed limiter and a gradient may leave you without the power to overtake safely.

On a motorway where there's long uphill gradients there may be a crawler lane. This type of lane helps the traffic to flow by diverting the slower heavy vehicles into an extra lane on the left.

Question

You're overtaking another LGV. Due to an uphill gradient you start to lose speed. You should

Mark one answer

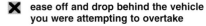

☒ **ease off and drop behind the vehicle you were attempting to overtake**

☒ continue at the same speed and position

☒ attempt to force the vehicle you were overtaking to drop back

☒ attempt to force the vehicle you were overtaking to speed up

If you attempt to overtake another vehicle and you realise that you're unable to complete the manoeuvre, ease off the accelerator and drop back behind the vehicle. If the vehicle you're attempting to overtake is large then it will take longer to pass. You should assess whether you have the time and the power to complete the manoeuvre before you attempt to overtake.

Question

After overtaking another PCV how would you know when it was safe to move back to the nearside lane?

Mark one answer

☒ **By relying on your own skill and judgement**

☒ By waiting for the driver you've just overtaken to flash the headlights

☒ By using your hazard warning lights as a signal

☒ By moving over to the nearside in the hope that the other vehicle will slow down

If you're driving a long vehicle you'll have to judge carefully when to pull back into the nearside lane after overtaking. Don't cut in on the vehicle you've overtaken – leave a safety margin. Check your left-hand (nearside) mirror to see whether the rear of your vehicle is well clear of the vehicle you've just passed. You should allow for the length of your vehicle and judge the manoeuvre accordingly. Don't rely on signals from other drivers. They may be signalling to someone else.

Question

You're turning right at a roundabout driving a long vehicle. You need to occupy the left-hand lane. You should check mirrors and

Mark one answer

☒ **signal right on approach**

☒ signal left on approach

☒ avoid giving a signal on approach

☒ signal right after entering the roundabout

There are times when, due to the size of your vehicle, you'll have to take up part of another lane. If you need to do this make sure that you use effective observation all around. Be aware that other road users might not understand the reasons for your position on the road. You should signal your intentions and take up your position in good time.

Question

With a long PCV, under normal driving conditions, when is it acceptable to straddle lanes?

Mark one answer

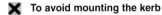

✗ To avoid mounting the kerb

✗ To stop other traffic from overtaking

✗ Always

✗ On the approach to all roundabouts

There are times when you might have to take up part of another lane in order to make a turn or manoeuvre. Be on your guard for other road users by using your mirrors to check all around your vehicle. Other traffic might try to move up alongside in the gap you've left to make your turn. Good planning and anticipation will allow you to signal your intentions to other road users and take up your position in good time.

This section looks at the effect of windy weather on
your vehicle.

The questions will ask you about

- High-sided vehicles

- Crosswinds

- Air deflectors

Question

When driving an empty curtain-sided vehicle how can you reduce crosswind problems?

Mark one answer

✖ Tie both curtain sides at one end of the vehicle

☒ Tie just one curtain side back and lock open the rear doors

☒ Leave both curtain sides closed

☒ Tie the curtain sides halfway back

If you're driving an empty vehicle that's curtain-sided you'll help lower the resistance to side winds if you tie back the curtains. The air will be able to flow across the flat bed of the vehicle and lessen any loss of control.

Question

You're driving an empty curtain-sided vehicle. Why should you tie the curtains open?

Mark one answer

✖ To reduce the effect of crosswinds

☒ To use less fuel

☒ It's a legal requirement

☒ To prevent the curtains tearing

Question

Drivers of LGVs fitted with curtain-sided bodies MUST ensure that

Mark one answer

✖ there will be no movement of the load in transit

☒ the heaviest items are positioned over the rear axle

☒ no hazardous chemicals are carried

☒ multi-drop loads are stowed in order of delivery

You must always ensure that any load you carry is secure and unlikely to move when in transit. This is essential when driving a curtain-sided vehicle as the curtains won't be strong enough to stop loose loads falling from the vehicle.

Question

High-sided vehicles can be affected by side winds.
In which TWO situations is this most likely?

Mark two answers

☒ **Open roads**

☒ **Motorway flyovers**

☒ Narrow country roads

☒ Motorway underpasses

☒ Built-up areas

☒ Roads with speed humps

Question

You're driving a high-sided vehicle in very windy conditions. Which TWO of the following should you avoid if possible?

Mark two answers

☒ **Suspension bridges**

☒ **Viaducts**

☒ Steep hills

☒ Country lanes

☒ Road tunnels

As a driver of a large vehicle you should listen to weather forecasts, which will tell you of any severe weather conditions. Plan your route accordingly. You're most likely to be subjected to high winds where there are

- high-level bridges
- high-level roads
- exposed viaducts
- exposed stretches of motorway

In windy weather try to avoid routes where you would have to negotiate these. Think about other factors that might lead to changes in route or rest periods, such as ferry cancellations.

Question

You're on a long journey. It starts to become windy and you're driving on an exposed road. What should you do?

Mark one answer

☒ **Try to find a less exposed route**

☒ Keep on driving

☒ Stop as soon as possible

☒ Inform the police

If you feel that the control of your vehicle is being affected by strong winds try to find a different route. This might add miles to your journey but could save fuel and reduce safety risks.

Question

In high winds, drivers of LGVs approaching high bridges or viaducts should expect

Mark three answers

☒ **lower speed limits**

☒ **lane closures**

☒ **diversions**

☐ minimum speed limits

☐ no restrictions for loaded vehicles

☐ no restrictions for LGVs

You might be delayed by road closures or diversions. Consider this when you're planning your rest stops. Delays will add to your driving time.

Question

Which of these vehicles is MOST at risk from high crosswinds?

Mark one answer

☒ **An unladen LGV with box body**

☐ A laden LGV with box body

☐ An unladen LGV with platform body

☐ A laden LGV with platform body

The combination of an unladen vehicle with high sides will leave it vulnerable to the effects of strong winds. An evenly distributed load will keep the vehicle more stable and less likely to be blown off course.

The higher your vehicle, the more it will be effected by strong winds. You must be prepared to retain control if it becomes unstable or difficult to control.

Question
Which TWO types of vehicle are most at risk
in windy conditions?

Mark two answers

☒ **High-sided LGVs**

☒ **Unladen vans**

☒ Saloon cars

☒ Single-decker buses

☒ Tractor units

The higher the sides of your vehicle, the
more the vehicle will be buffeted by strong
winds. The large area of bodywork will
present a resistance to crosswinds and this
in turn will affect the control you have on
the vehicle. The risk of loss of control will be
increased if your vehicle isn't carrying a load.
The vehicle will be lighter and so could be
more easily pushed off course by the wind.

Question
Double-deck PCVs are more likely than
single-deck PCVs to be affected by

Mark one answer

☒ **strong winds**

☒ heavy rain

☒ thick fog

☒ dense spray

If you're driving a double-decker bus you'll
feel the effect of the wind to a greater
degree, due to the vehicle's extra height.

Question
What is a 'buffer' lane?

Mark one answer

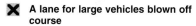 **A lane for large vehicles blown off course**

A lane for overtaking

A lane to park in until the wind drops

The only lane to be used in high winds

Question
In high winds where would you expect to find 'buffer' lanes?

Mark one answer

 **On high bridges**

In built-up areas

On country roads

In roadworks

Question
When is a 'buffer' lane most likely to be in use?

Mark one answer

When windy

When raining

When foggy

When icy

During high winds one of the lanes on high bridges might be closed to traffic to create a 'buffer' lane. This lane is kept free to prevent vehicles being blown into the path of other road users in the next lane.

The closure of this lane may cause traffic congestion and delay. If your route takes in any locations that are frequently subjected to high winds such as

- high-level bridges
- high-level roads
- exposed viaducts
- exposed stretches of motorway

listen to the weather forecasts, which will inform you of the need to replan your route.

A buffer lane is established when the wind begins to cause a risk to high-sided vehicles. At other times it will be a normal lane. Don't use the buffer lane unless your vehicle has been blown off course into it, or you need to use it to avoid an accident. Leave it free, however busy the traffic.

Question

Which of these vehicles is most at risk from strong crosswinds on motorways?

Mark one answer

☒ **A motorcycle**

☒ An unladen LGV

☒ A sports car

☒ A road tanker

Question

In strong winds an overtaking LGV can affect other road users.
Which vehicle is most at risk?

Mark one answer

☒ **A motorcycle**

☒ A car

☒ A furniture van

☒ A coach

Question

Which THREE of the following vehicles are most likely to be affected by high winds?

Mark three answers

☒ **Cyclists**

☒ **Vehicles towing caravans**

☒ **Curtain-sided vehicles**

☒ Track-laying vehicles

☒ Front-wheel-drive vehicles

☒ Slow-moving vehicles

Motorcyclists overtaking high-sided vehicles experience a drop in pressure when they're alongside and protected from side winds. This can cause them to veer to one side. The effect will be reversed when they complete the manoeuvre and emerge again from the shelter of the bigger vehicle.

On motorways there may be exposed stretches of road where there are strong crosswinds. A gust of wind might blow the motorcycle across the lane, or the rider might experience buffeting when overtaking or being overtaken. If you're following or are alongside a motorcyclist you should be aware that the weather will also affect the control of the motorcycle.

Other road users such as cyclists could be blown off course by high winds. You should be aware of this when you're following or planning to overtake them. Vehicles that are towing caravans can also feel the effect of high winds, to a degree where it might blow them off course.

If you're driving a curtain-sided vehicle in very windy weather it's safer to secure both curtain sides at one end of the vehicle. This cuts down the wind resistance and lessens the risk of being blown off course.

Question
As a PCV driver which TWO of the following should you do when overtaking a motorcyclist in strong winds?

Mark two answers

- ☒ **Use the nearside mirror**
- ☒ **Pass wide**
- ☐ Sound the horn
- ☐ Pass close
- ☐ Move back in early

You should always check your nearside mirror as you overtake. If you're overtaking a motorcyclist and the weather is windy, pass them leaving plenty of room, as the rider might wobble or swerve.

Question
You're overtaking a motorcycle in windy conditions.
Why should you always check your nearside mirror?

Mark one answer

- ☒ **To see if the rider is still in control of the motorcycle**
- ☐ To check your road position
- ☐ To see if other vehicles have been affected
- ☐ To check if it's properly adjusted

You must check the nearside mirror before, during and after overtaking a motorcyclist. Make sure that the rider is still in control and that the size of your vehicle hasn't caused buffeting.

Question
When are air deflectors most effective?

Mark one answer

- ☒ **When there's a head wind**
- ☐ When there's a crosswind
- ☐ When reversing
- ☐ When there's a strong tail wind

Cab-mounted air deflectors and lower panels will streamline the vehicle and therefore offer less resistance to the air around it. This will decrease the vehicle's fuel consumption, and we should all be concerned with the conservation of fuel. This aim is linked not only to financial issues, although important, but it's allied to environmental conservation as well. Conserving energy and resources should be a concern for all drivers on the road.

SECTION 12 | HEAVY RAIN

This section looks at the effects of heavy rain.

The questions will ask you about

- Splashing spray

- Saturated roads

Question

In heavy rain what's the least amount of space you should allow for braking?

Mark one answer

✖ Twice the normal distance

☒ The normal distance

☒ Three times the normal distance

☒ Five times the normal distance

Your tyres could lose their grip in wet conditions. If you're travelling in heavy rain you should be aware that it could take twice as long for you to stop as in dry weather. Therefore increase your distance from the vehicle in front.

Question

You're driving on a motorway. Your view ahead is poor due to heavy spray.
Which THREE of the following should you do?

Mark three answers

✖ Use the four-second rule

✖ Use your dipped headlights

✖ Reduce your speed

☒ Use your full-beam headlights

☒ Use the lane to the right

If you're travelling on a motorway and your view ahead is poor then you should reduce your speed. Leave about four seconds between you and the vehicle in front, and make sure that others can see you by using your dipped headlights.

Question

Before braking in wet conditions you should make sure, as far as possible, that

Mark one answer

✖ your vehicle is travelling in a straight line

☒ the gear lever is in neutral

☒ all spray-suppression equipment is working

☒ there's no mist on your rear mirror

If you need to brake when the road surface is wet, do so while your vehicle is travelling in a straight line. This will lessen the risk of skidding. As a professional driver you should be in the routine of braking in good time, so that you aren't braking and steering at the same time.

Question

What causes extra danger when overtaking in rain?

Mark one answer

☒ **Spray from large vehicles**

☒ Other vehicles driving slowly

☒ Vehicles wandering off

☒ Increase in vehicle noise

Other vehicles might create a heavy spray so you must be cautious when you're overtaking. Severe spray can result in a loss of visibility as you overtake. Be aware of this and anticipate it happening.

Spray from your vehicle could cause the driver of an overtaking vehicle to lose visibility. You should be aware of this as smaller vehicles overtake you.

Question

You intend to overtake a large vehicle that's throwing up spray. You should

Mark one answer

☒ **move out earlier than normal**

☒ get much closer before moving out

☒ wait until the other driver gives a left signal

☒ wait for the other vehicle to slow down on a hill

If you wish to overtake a vehicle that's throwing up spray move out to overtake earlier than normal. This will prevent you being affected by the rear spray as well as the side spray as you pass.

Question

You're driving a PCV in the rain. When overtaking a cyclist extra care has to be taken because of

Mark one answer

☒ **spray from your vehicle**

☒ wind from your vehicle

☒ noise from your vehicle

☒ the size of your vehicle

When passing other road users, especially motorcyclists and cyclists, the spray from your vehicle could affect their control. Pass them leaving plenty of room, and check in your left-hand mirror as you pass to see whether they're still in control.

Question

Spray-suppression equipment fitted to PCVs is particularly useful when it's

Mark one answer

✗ raining

☒ icy

☒ foggy

☒ windy

If there's heavy rain the suppression equipment fitted on your vehicle will protect other road users from loss of visibility when following or passing your vehicle. Check the wheel arches to ensure that the fitments haven't worked loose or that any parts haven't broken off. Well-maintained equipment will force the spray back down onto the road instead of to the rear and the sides of the vehicle.

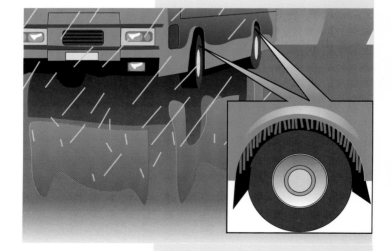

This book is intended to help you to prepare for the LGV or PCV theory test. If you've prepared properly and fully you won't find your question paper difficult.

Sitting your theory test means that you've taken the first step towards driving as a vocation. Passing the theory test, however, is only one stage in becoming a safe and competent professional driver. The knowledge you've learned should be put into practice on the road. By passing a stringent, two-part test and continuing to apply the knowledge that you've gained on the way you can make an important contribution to safe driving on our roads.

You'll never know all the answers. Throughout your driving career there will always be more to learn. Remember, the passengers or goods you carry will be your responsibility. But by being reliable, efficient and safe you'll be on your way to becoming a good professional driver.

Service standards for theory test candidates

The DSA and the DVTA are committed to providing the following standards of service for test candidates.

Theory tests will be available

- During weekdays, evenings and on Saturdays. A test appointment should be available for 95% of test candidates within two weeks

- Test notification will be issued within five working days of receipt of a correctly completed application form and appropriate fee

- 95% of telephone calls will be answered within ten seconds

- More time may be needed to make arrangements for candidates with special needs, but a test should be available for 95% of such candidates within four weeks

- Refund of test fees will be issued within three weeks of a valid claim with the supporting information

- All letters, including complaints, will be answered within 15 working days

- All candidates should be able to obtain a test booking at their preferred test session within two months of their preferred date and the centre of their choice

- No more than 0.5% of tests will be cancelled by *DriveSafe Ltd* (acting on behalf of the DSA and the DVTA)

Complaints guide for theory test candidates

The DSA and the DVTA aim to give their customers the best possible service. Please tell us

- When we've done well
- When you aren't satisfied

Your comments can help us to improve the service we offer. If you have any questions about your theory test please contact 01203 662 600.

If you have any complaints about how your theory test was carried out, or any part of our customer service, please take up the matter with a member of staff if the circumstances allow. You may complete a form, available at theory test centres. Alternatively you can write to the Head of Central Services at the following address

Head of Central Services
Driving Theory Test
PO Box 445
Coventry CV1 2ZZ
Tel: 01203 241 130
Fax: 01203 632 680

If you're dissatisfied with the reply you can write to the Managing Director at the same address.

If you're still not satisfied, you can take up your complaint with

The Chief Executive
Driving Standards Agency
Stanley House
Talbot Street
Nottingham NG1 5GU

In Northern Ireland

The Chief Executive
Driver and Vehicle Licensing Agency
Balmoral Road
Belfast BT12 6QL

None of this removes your right to take your complaint to your Member of Parliament, who may decide on your case personally with the Chief Executive, the Minister or the Parliamentary Commissioner for Administration (the Ombudsman).

Before doing this you should seek legal advice.

Compensation code for theory test candidates

The DSA will normally refund the test
fee, or give a free re-booking, in the
following cases

- If we cancel your test

- If you cancel and give us at least
  three working days' notice

- If you keep the test appointment
  but the test doesn't take place,
  or isn't finished, for a reason that
  isn't your fault

We'll also repay you the expenses
that you incurred on the day of the
test because we cancelled your test
at short notice. We'll consider
reasonable claims for

- Travelling to and from the
  test centre

- Any pay or earnings you lost after
  tax (usually for half a day)

Please write to the office where you
booked your test and send a receipt
showing travel costs and/or an
employer's letter, which shows what
earnings you lost.

The DVTA has a different
compensation code. If you think
you're entitled to compensation
apply to the centre where you booked
your test.

**This compensation code doesn't
affect your existing legal rights.**

Printed in the United Kingdon for The Stationery Office
Dd 0000000, 12/96, C125, 000000, 00000